Historical Evidence and the Reading of Seventeenth-Century Poetry

Historical Evidence and the Reading of Seventeenth-Century Poetry 🐾

Cleanth Brooks

University of Missouri Press

Columbia and London

Copyright © 1991 by
The Curators of the University of Missouri
University of Missouri Press, Columbia, Missouri 65201
Printed and bound in the United States of America
5   4   3   2   1   95   94   93   92   91

Library of Congress Cataloging-in-Publication Data

Brooks, Cleanth, 1906–
    Historical evidence and the reading of seventeenth-century
    poetry / Cleanth Brooks.
        p.   cm.
    Includes bibliographical references and index.
    ISBN 0–8262–0775–8
    1. English poetry—Early modern, 1500–1700—History and
criticism. 2. Historical criticism (Literature)—England.
3. History in literature. I. Title.
PR545.H5B7   1991
821'.709358—dc20   90–25397
                                                       CIP

∞™ This paper meets the requirements of the
American National Standard for Permanence of Paper
for Printed Library Materials, Z39.48, 1984.

Designer: Rhonda Gibson
Typesetter: Connell-Zeko Type & Graphics
Printer: Thomson-Shore, Inc.
Binder: Thomson-Shore, Inc.
Typeface: Sabon

In memory of David Nichol Smith

Contents

Historical Evidence
and the
Reading of
Seventeenth-Century Poetry

Introduction

The notion that Clio, the Muse of History, has a quarrel with her sister muses goes on vociferously. It is, however, a modern invention. Neither Hesiod nor any other of the ancient authorities refers to a tiff among the sisterhood. The Olympian gods, according to Homer, were often at odds with one another, but Homer doesn't speak of any contention among the muses.

Nevertheless, some of their later devotees have set up their own bickering factions, though there are surely no real grounds for jealous conflict between the proponents of history and those who are primarily concerned with what used to be called belles lettres. The activities they practice are in fact thoroughly compatible and often mutually supportive. Sometimes the biographer, the literary historian, and the lexicographer hold the keys necessary for unlocking a poem's full meaning, especially if the poem dates from an earlier time. We must remember, however, that such information as the biographer or historian can provide cannot in itself determine literary value. Often it cannot even fully determine meaning. A mediocre or even worthless poem (or novel or play) may profit from, and even require, as much help from the biographer or literary historian as a work of great literary value. Dates are dates, facts are facts, whether they have to do with the popular American ballad "Casey Jones," Longfellow's *Hiawatha,* or Keats's magnificent "Ode to a Nightingale."

Generalizations of this sort may seem too extreme for ready acceptance, and I admit that I have stated matters in oversimple terms. But rather than try at this point to state in more general and abstract terms the relevant applications, reservations, and qualifications, I propose to offer in the chapters that follow what might be regarded as several case histories, concrete discussions of some dozen poems. One could have illustrated the relations of historical background and critical assessment by using stories, plays, or novels, but to do this adequately would call for an oversized volume. Poems are more concentrated and concise. I have deliberately limited my examples to one cultural period, specifi-

1

cally the period extending from the early years of the seventeenth century and ending in 1663. (Other fifty-year periods might have served as
well, and I was seriously tempted to choose poems printed between
1840 and 1890.)

No literary period, of course, is truly homogeneous. The works I
shall discuss represent varying talents, interests, ideas, and conventions.
Yet all the poets of the first half of the seventeenth century were much
alike in their education, ideas, beliefs, and in the literary models they
followed. Such general likeness is enhanced by the fact that, of the nine
poets principally discussed, eight were minor poets, and all these eight
were Royalists. Even the one exception, Andrew Marvell, began his
career with strong Royalist connections and sympathies. He is an exception, too, in literary rank, for he is "minor" only in that he attempted no
major work.

My choice of minor figures is also deliberate. Minor poets are less
likely than their greater contemporaries to go beyond, or deviate from, a
period style.

Though I am here principally interested in literary criticism, I want at
the outset to stress my own belief in the importance of biographical-
historical information for the elucidation of a literary document. On
occasion, such information may indeed provide the only way for arriv-
ing at the meaning.

In Samuel Butler's *Hudibras,* part 1, canto 1, the poet, probably
echoing a passage in Cervantes's *Don Quixote,* comments on the odd
fact that there is so little on record about the diet of the knights errant of
the romances. That lack of reference, he tells us, has caused some unwary writers to claim that Arthur's knights had "no stomach, but to
fight." This notion the poet proceeds to demolish.

> 'Tis false: for *Arthur* wore in Hall
> Round-Table like a farthingal,
> On which, with shirt pull'd out behind
> And eke before, his good Knights din'd
> Tho' twas no Table some suppose,
> But a huge pair of round Trunk-hose:
> In which he carry'd as much meat
> As he and all his Knights could eat, . . .
>   (lines 337–44)

Butler's display of erudition is, of course, mock learning. Nobody
ever had put King Arthur into a kind of spreading petticoat or into

trunkhose, and today Butler's jest seems a particularly pointless one. It is certainly puzzling, but Butler's editors, down to the present day, have not been able to throw any light on the passage.

Many years ago I happened to acquire an edition of *Hudibras* published in 1793. It is a fine quarto handsomely printed on thick paper and with wide margins. The editor was the Reverend Treadway Russel Nash, an accomplished eighteenth-century antiquary. Since Nash was a friend of Bishop Thomas Percy, whose correspondence I was helping to edit, and since the copy was advertised as the editor's personal copy, I bought it, hoping to find marginalia having to do with Percy's antiquarian activities.

In that matter I was disappointed, but the several volumes proved very interesting in themselves. After his edition had been published, Nash had been able to find further information. So he wrote a few notes and comments on the flyleaves or on notepaper neatly inserted to face the relevant passage. He also loosely inserted in the volume the original drawings from which the handsome copperplates had been made. Yet when it came to the passage on Arthur's Round Table, all that Nash had been able to do was to supply brief accounts of *farthingale* and *trunk-hose* and an interesting note in which he quotes the speech of True-wit (a character in Ben Jonson's *Epicene, or the Silent Woman,* first acted in 1609) in which True-wit says of another character in the play, Sir Amorous La-Foole, "If he could but victual himself for half a year in his breeches, he is sufficiently armed to over-run a country" (act 4, scene 5). Evidently early in the century there was a good deal of jesting about trunkhose as an article of dress and about the absurd size of some that were worn.

It should be noted that in a passage that occurs a few lines before the Round Table passage, Butler tells us that Sir Hudibras, the anti-hero of this satire, had lined his woolen breeches

> with many a piece
> Of Amunition-Bread and Cheese,
> And fat black puddings, proper food
> For Warriors that delight in blood.
> For, as we said, He alwaies chose
> To carry vittles in his hose.
>
> (lines 313–18)

So Sir Hudibras was accustomed to do what King Arthur is said to have done but, according to our poet, the king outdid him. His trunk-

hose not only contained plentiful food for his knights' feasts but constituted the very table around which they sat to eat it.

We do not know in what year Nash discovered the solution to his problem, but clearly it was some time after his handsome edition had been printed. For in his own copy he has inserted opposite the passage in question an extra leaf on which he pasted a crude woodcut of Arthur's round table. This was extracted from a copy of *The Most Ancient and Famous History of the renowned Prince Arthur, King of Britaine, wherein is declared his Life and Death, with all his glorious Battailes against the Saxons, Saracens and Pagans, which (for the honour of his Country) he most worthily achieved. As also, all the Noble Acts, and Heroicke Deeds of his Valiant Knights of the Round Table. Newly refined and published for the delight and profit of the Reader.*

The text is in three parts, the woodcut being repeated as the frontispiece of each part. The book was published in London, printed by William Stansby for Jacob Bloome, 1634. It is No. 806 in the *Short Title Catalogue*.

As the reader will see, the woodcut shows how Arthur solved the problem of no precedence. The king's head and upper body seem to protrude from a hole cut in the middle of the table, no one sits on his right hand or his left, and if only he had been provided with a modern swivel chair he could at will have looked, eye to eye, at any of his fourteen knights that sit around the table. But how he got into his hole in the center of the table, the ingenious contriver of the woodcut has left to the reader's imagination.

I assume that Butler had seen this grotesque woodcut, and had noted that the table as portrayed does make it look as if Arthur is wearing a monstrous farthingale. Evidently Butler decided to share his amusement with his readers. But how many of them could he count upon to have seen the woodcut? It is hard to say, though some of the available evidence would suggest that the book was widely circulated. After all, it was a seventeenth-century reprint of Malory's famous *Le Morte Darthur*. The text was set up in blackletter, the typeface in which older and familiar books such as the Bible as well as popular tales that appealed to the folk continued to be printed long after books intended for the better educated were printed in Roman type. Some years ago when Maggs Brothers advertised a copy for sale they did not label it "rare" or even "scarce." Perhaps many people did see the woodcut. But whether many or few, an understanding of the joke demands that the reader should have seen that same woodcut.

At this point, the reader of this Introduction may feel that, even so, the passage isn't very funny. If this is his reaction, I share it fully with him. The reader may also feel that working out the problem wasn't worth the trouble. Perhaps not. But an editor is committed to solving the problems set by his text, and without such elucidation the text here in question doesn't make sense. As for trouble, it cost me no trouble at all. It was a case of pure serendipity. I was looking for something else when I stumbled upon an eighteenth-century scholar's discovery.

Moreover, I take it that to Nash himself the solution came as a complete surprise. He had already spent, one supposes, considerable labor in combing the literature of the period for a possible explanation—for such a reference as he had turned up in Ben Jonson's play. But surely he didn't deliberately seek out a copy of *The Most Ancient and Famous History* with any expectation of finding his answer there.

In short, for some problems, sweat and toil do not avail: some exegetical discoveries are made by accident. A second and more important point to be made is related to the first: the difficulty required to find a solution is not necessarily a measure of its importance—historical or literary. Poor literary work, I repeat, may be as difficult to interpret as good. In fact, the greater literary works, in spite of their richness of meaning, often do, as T. S. Eliot wrote long ago, communicate before they are fully understood.

A third point is so obvious as to be hardly worth specific notice. Literary works that depend upon special references will usually require of a later audience much biographical-historical help. Thus, satire is notorious for the difficulty it offers to readers of a later century. For instance, the modern reader recognizes few of the fools and knaves pilloried in Pope's *Dunciad*. If he really wants to know who they are, he will have to read a great many scholarly footnotes. The fact that *Hudibras* is a satire accounts in good part for the difficulty of many of its allusions. In any case, the spirit of this poem is that of a lark, a romp, an outrageous caricature. Anything, or almost anything, goes, and there seems to be no special catering on Butler's part for such of his readers as were not "in the know."

To the reader of a later generation, of course, all the literature of the past, whether satiric or not, will appear to have been written for "insiders." As outsiders, readers of our own century may require considerable help with the poems to be discussed in the chapters that follow, for the most recent of these poems was written more than three hundred years ago.

Yet none of them sets a problem so special as that in the passage I have quoted from *Hudibras*. I chose the passage deliberately as the most extreme instance I could find of a nearly absolute dependence of literary criticism upon historical information. I trust that it may stand as an emphatic acknowledgment on my part of the importance and sometimes complete necessity for scholarly help.

For my purposes in this book it can serve as a sort of benchmark. All the poems to be discussed in subsequent pages require far less biographical-historical information, but all, I should think, will require some. Because they all reflect in one way or other the cultural matrix out of which they came—that of the Jacobean-Caroline era—an examination of them as literary entities as well as cultural products of the same historical period might conceivably throw some light on the relationship of scholarship as strictly interpreted to literary criticism proper. After the past two generations of heated debate, more light would be welcome.

I

The Poet's Sincerity

Henry King

An Exequy. To his Matchlesse never to be forgotten Freind

Accept, thou Shrine of my Dead Saint!
Instead of Dirges this Complaint;
And, for sweet flowres to crowne thy Hearse,
Receive a strew of weeping verse
From thy griev'd Friend; whome Thou might'st see   5
Quite melted into Teares for Thee.
    Deare Losse! since thy untimely fate
My task hath beene to meditate
On Thee, on Thee: Thou art the Book,
The Library whereon I look   10
Though almost blind. For Thee (Lov'd Clay!)
I Languish out, not Live the Day,
Using no other Exercise
But what I practise with mine Eyes.
By which wett glasses I find out   15
How lazily Time creepes about
To one that mournes: This, only This
My Exercise and bus'nes is:
So I compute the weary howres
With Sighes dissolved into Showres.   20
    Nor wonder if my time goe thus
Backward and most praeposterous;
Thou hast Benighted mee. Thy Sett
This Eve of blacknes did begett,
Who wast my Day, (though overcast   25
Before thou hadst thy Noon-tide past)
And I remember must in teares,
Thou scarce hadst seene so many Yeeres
As Day tells Howres. By thy cleere Sunne

7

My Love and Fortune first did run;   30
But Thou wilt never more appeare
Folded within my Hemispheare:
Since both thy Light and Motion
Like a fledd Starr is fall'n and gone;
And 'twixt mee and my Soule's deare wish   35
The Earth now interposed is,
Which such a straunge Ecclipse doth make
As ne're was read in Almanake.
   I could allow Thee for a time
To darken mee and my sad Clime,   40
Were it a Month, a Yeere, or Ten,
I would thy Exile live till then;
And all that space my mirth adjourne,
So thou wouldst promise to returne,
And putting off thy ashy Shrowd   45
At length disperse this Sorrowe's Cloud.
   But woe is mee! the longest date
Too narrowe is to calculate
These empty hopes. Never shall I
Be so much blest, as to descry   50
A glympse of Thee, till that Day come
Which shall the Earth to cinders doome,
And a fierce Feaver must calcine
The Body of this World, like Thine,
(My Little World!) That fitt of Fire   55
Once off, our Bodyes shall aspire
To our Soules' blisse: Then wee shall rise,
And view our selves with cleerer eyes
In that calme Region, where no Night
Can hide us from each other's sight.   60
   Meane time, thou hast Hir Earth: Much good
May my harme doe thee. Since it stood
With Heaven's will I might not call
Hir longer Mine; I give thee all
My short liv'd right and Interest   65
In Hir, whome living I lov'd best:
With a most free and bounteous grief,
I give thee what I could not keep.
Be kind to Hir: and prethee look
Thou write into thy Doomsday book   70
Each parcell of this Rarity,
Which in thy Caskett shrin'd doth ly:

See that thou make thy reck'ning streight,
And yeeld Hir back againe by weight;
For thou must Auditt on thy trust 75
Each Grane and Atome of this Dust:
As thou wilt answere Him, that leant,
Not gave thee, my deare Monument.
   So close the ground, and 'bout hir shade
Black Curtaines draw, My Bride is lay'd 80
   Sleep on (my Love!) in thy cold bed
Never to be disquieted.
My last Good-night! Thou wilt not wake
Till I Thy Fate shall overtake:
Till age, or grief, or sicknes must 85
Marry my Body to that Dust
It so much loves; and fill the roome
My heart keepes empty in Thy Tomb.
Stay for mee there: I will not faile
To meet Thee in that hollow Vale. 90
And think not much of my delay;
I am already on the way,
And follow Thee with all the speed
Desire can make, or Sorrowes breed.
Each Minute is a short Degree 95
And e'ry Howre a stepp towards Thee.
At Night when I betake to rest,
Next Morne I rise neerer my West
Of Life, almost by eight Howres' sayle,
Then when Sleep breath'd his drowsy gale. 100
   Thus from the Sunne my Bottome steares,
And my Daye's Compasse downward beares.
Nor labour I to stemme the Tide,
Through which to Thee I swiftly glide.
   'Tis true; with shame and grief I yeild 105
Thou, like the Vanne, first took'st the Field,
And gotten hast the Victory
In thus adventuring to Dy
Before Mee; whose more yeeres might crave
A just præcedence in the Grave. 110
But hark! My Pulse, like a soft Drum
Beates my Approach, Tells Thee I come;
And, slowe howe're my Marches bee,
I shall at last sitt downe by Thee.
   The thought of this bids mee goe on, 115

And wait my dissolution
With Hope and Comfort. Deare! (forgive
The Crime) I am content to live
Divided, with but half a Heart,
Till we shall Meet and Never part.

"An Exequy" is a poem on the death of Bishop Henry King's wife in 1624. The poem has elicited high praise from poets as radically different as T. S. Eliot and Edgar Allan Poe. Eliot regarded lines 111–12, in which the mourning husband says to the dead wife, "But hark! My pulse, like a soft Drum, / Beates my Approach, Tells Thee I come," as constituting one of the finest examples of the metaphysical conceit. Poe, of course, could be expected to like "The Exequy" if for no other reason than for its subject matter, the death of a beautiful and beloved woman. After all, Poe's own showpiece is "The Raven," in which a lover mourns the death of his lost Lenore.

King also apparently had a liking for poems of this sort. He wrote many laments and elegies, but there have been few to praise them. Why, then, does King's masterpiece so far surpass his other poems in this genre? The question is a pertinent one, for "The Exequy" employs much the same literary conventions, rhetorical devices, and "conceited" imagery that characterize all of King's funereal verse. Many readers will declare that the obvious answer is that King was deeply and sincerely grieved at the loss of his wife, Anne, whereas he merely followed the polite conventions when he expressed a formal sorrow in "An Elegy Upon the immature losse of the most vertuous Lady Anne Riche," or in "An Elegy Upon Mrs. Kirk unfortunately Drowned in Thames." "The Exequy," so this argument would run, is the outcome of genuine emotion. After all, what was Lady Anne Rich to him? Or he to Mistress Kirk?

In a rough and ready fashion, such a way of accounting for the superior merit of "The Exequy" makes a certain sense, though the truth is that the biographers and literary historians can tell us absolutely nothing about the relations of our poet to any of these three esteemed ladies. We possess no real evidence. We say that we simply "know" from reading "The Exequy" that the grief is real and from reading the other two poems that it is not. But the argument here is clearly circular: our only basis for judging the sincerity of the poems is the character of the poems themselves.

Thus, what we should be asking is this: what is there in the makeup of "The Exequy" that convinces us that the sentiments expressed are authentic? But there is a further point: the sincerity of the author even when demonstrable by biographical evidence doesn't guarantee poetic virtue. The skeptic on this point may be referred to the agony column of the average city newspaper. You can't convince me that the sorrowing mother who begins "'Tis one year and a day / Since our little Willie passed away" simply could not be expressing a heartfelt sorrow. Even the professional poet wracked by genuine grief is capable of shameless tear-jerking. James Russell Lowell's "After the Burial"—though it contains some beautiful lines—will make the point. Thus, if most readers of "The Exequy" feel that it expresses genuine sorrow, that belief must be no more than an inference from the poem itself. It is for such reasons as the foregoing that I think that we shall have to seek the poetic merit of "The Exequy" in what it is able to convey to the reader, both explicitly and by implication.

The structure of the poem lives up to its title. The word *exequy* means funeral rite, and ultimately derives from the Latin *exequi,* "to follow out," and, as the *OED* expands it, to "follow to the grave." Such is the framework of the poem. As the poem opens, the funeral procession has evidently reached the already open grave. The bereaved husband now lays on his wife's bier "a strew of weeping verse" rather than the usual cluster of "sweet flowres." The first sixty lines of the poem are addressed to her, whereas lines 61–78 are addressed to the earth, which is to receive her body.

In "The Exequy" King makes use of the literary conventions and the witty imagery and verbal wordplay of the time. He may seem to be beginning his poem with a flourish of mere rhetorical extravagance: he addresses his dead wife as a "saint" as he lays his poem as an offering on her "shrine." But a more careful reading makes it plain that, in fact, the husband has not claimed canonization for his wife nor established for her, even in metaphor, an ornate shrine such as befits a medieval saint. Nor is he likening himself to a pilgrim come to pay his devotion and veneration to the holy relics enclosed.

He is much more modest in all his claims. The bereft husband is here addressing the *body* of his dead wife. The shrine in question is her body. He calls it a shrine because it once contained her spirit (as a medieval shrine contains the bones or other relics of a saint). In doing this, he is drawing on the familiar Christian concept of the body as the temple of the holy ghost, the earthly case containing the immortal soul. Shakespeare makes use of the same concept in Sonnet 146 when he writes, "Poor soul, the center of my sinful earth." In calling his wife a "saint," King is using the term to signify the devout and committed Christian.

Such usage was general at the time. Milton was, a few years later, to use *saint* in just this sense in the sonnet in which he refers to his dead wife as "my late espoused saint." That the shrine referred to in the first line of King's poem is indeed the dead body is confirmed by line 11, in which he addresses her body as "Lov'd Clay."

It is true that he addresses the inanimate remains as if the dead woman were still able to hear him. But this notion hardly transcends accepted usage. Traditional verse and prose have, for centuries, been full of anguished lovers speaking to the loved one's corpse as if it still contained the breath of life. Even so, the poet does not press the issue here, for in writing "Thou might'st see [me] / Quite melted into Teares for Thee" (lines 5–6), he uses the conditional, not the indicative "Thou mayst see," for he well knows that the dead eyes cannot see anything.

The word *glasses* in line 15 (where he refers to his eyes as "wett glasses") perhaps requires a gloss. Though in the seventeenth century *glasses* could refer as now to telescopes and spectacles, the word could also signify the unaided eyes themselves, and such has to be the meaning here.

The mourner goes on the say that through his tear-blinded eyes—because of their blurred vision, or in spite of it?—he finds out

> How lazily Time creepes about
> To one that mournes.
> (lines 16–17)

He goes further: time is not merely slowed; it actually runs "Backward and most praeposterous" (line 22). King is using *preposterous* in its precise, etymological sense (hindside-before), though by the seventeenth century the present meaning (absurd, ridiculous) had already developed.

The mourning husband reflects that it is no wonder that his sense of time is confused, for in losing his wife he has lost the "cleere Sunne" of his life (line 29). Therefore, he finds himself, even in broad daylight, benighted, encompassed in an "Eve of blacknes" (line 24).

In fact, the course of his sun has run contrary to normal expectations, for it has now set beneath earth's rim before it had ever reached its full "Noon-tide" (line 26). The husband presses this circumstance of early and untimely death further still, with the implication that his wife had scarcely completed her full day, for he remarks in lines 28–29,

> Thou scarce hadst seene so many Yeeres
> As Day tells [that is, numbers] Howres.

Here the historian can confirm the implication, for the scant records we possess indicate that Anne King was not quite twenty-four when she died. So the allusion seems neat and precise. This kind of detail in their figurative language is, of course, the hallmark of the great metaphysicals.

King goes on to develop further the sun figure. His sun has set, but, unlike that other sun that, by reappearing every morning, brings light and warmth to mankind in general, his cannot be expected to return to him. So he finds a more accurate and mournful analogy for her departure: not in our great daystar, but in a shooting star that, after a brief transit across the sky, falls to earth and loses its light forever.

With line 35, the poet shifts to still another metaphorical description of what has befallen his sun. It has suffered eclipse—an unexpected and therefore shocking eclipse, since no "Almanake" had predicted it. The poet makes his figurative language reflect the very mechanism of an eclipse.

> . . . 'twixt mee and my Soule's deare wish
> The Earth now interposed is.
> (lines 35–36)

This sounds like an eclipse of the moon in which earth's shadow blots out the moon's light. If the eclipse is that of the sun, it is the moon that interposes itself between the sun and the observer. (Several of the manuscripts actually read "An Earth." The moon as a planetary body of the order of the earth might indeed be called "an earth.")

Yet whether the eclipse is that of the sun or the moon, the point of the figure offered is the same: the grieving lover will be left in lasting darkness, for he has no hope of any recovery of the wished-for light. Indeed, he says that if he only knew that in ten years his light would return, he might be able to endure his present state. But it may be eons before his light will put "off [her] ashy Shrowd" (line 45).

For the modern reader lines 47–48, "But woe is mee! the longest date / Too narrowe is to calculate," may require a note. "Date" here means "duration" (*OED* 4). Thus, "the longest duration" or period of time is too brief even to calculate her hoped-for return. In fact, he cannot expect to see her until the end of the world, when the earth and all that is in it, including her dead body and his, shall be burnt to ashes.

The belief that the world would be destroyed by fire rests principally upon one of the minor books of the New Testament, 2 Peter 3:10. The King James version, which is presumably the one that Bishop King used, reads as follows: "But the day of the Lord will come as a thief in the night; in which the heavens shall pass away with a great noise, and the elements shall melt with fervent heat, the earth also and the works that are therein shall be burned up."

In lines 53–54 the speaker tells us that a "fierce Feaver" brought about the death of his wife, and he now makes plain that such a fever will, in the last days, bring to an end the life of the world itself. (Thus, the fate of Anne as microcosm looks toward a similar fate of the macrocosm. He calls his wife in line 55 "My Little World.")

Yet, once this "fitt of Fire" (line 55) is over, the mourner and his wife will rise phoenix-like from their ashes. (Though King does not directly invoke the phoenix image, it clearly underlies the passage.) Moreover, it is implied that the action of the fire is cleansing and purifying, for they will arise from their dust and look upon each other with "cleerer eyes" in a realm of everlasting day in which "no Night / Can hide [them] from each other's sight" (lines 59–60).

Though again King does not spell out the precise way in which the dead shall arise from their graves, he apparently believes that the grains of dust or ashes will be reconstituted to become the resurrected body. Such a view was common in the period. King's contemporary and friend, Izaac Walton, expresses the same belief in his biography of another contemporary and friend of King's, John Donne. I quote the last sentence of Walton's "Life of Donne": "That body . . . / is now become a small quantity / of Christian dust, but I shall see it reanimated." In short, King's conception is not at all that envisaged in Shelley's line "like a ghost from the tomb," but that of a literal reading of the Apostles' Creed: "I believe . . . in the resurrection of the body."

At line 61 the speaker, with a distinct shift in his tone, now addresses himself to the earth that will, with the lowering of Anne's body into the grave, take possession of it. But not forever. The speaker reminds the earth that some day it will be required to

> . . . yeeld Hir back againe by weight;
> For thou must Auditt on thy trust
> Each Grane and Atome of this Dust.
>   (lines 74–76)

The tone of his admonition to the earth lies somewhere between resignation and bitter reproach. It is the tone of a man who has had to give up, through some mishap or turn of fortune, a precious possession into the hands of another. It is his bitterness that is uppermost in "Much good / May my harme doe thee" (lines 61–62); his resignation, in "I give thee what I could not keep" (line 68); and a touchingly desperate appeal to the new possessor's unlikely good nature in "Be kind to Hir" (line 69). The last tonal shift is to a note of grim warning. God has merely lent, not given, the beloved body to the earth, and on his great day he will demand a strict accounting of his property and a full return of every particle of it.

The phrase "thy Doomsday book" (line 70) is very effective here. The detailed inventory of all the land and real property in England, which William the Conqueror ordered to be made in 1086, had long become a byword for any thorough and detailed accounting. The great inventory was known as the Domesday Book because it provided the final judgment (doom) on all matters that came within its scope or reference. But in King's time "doom's day" had, of course, also come to name the last great Judgment Day, in which the Lord shall raise the dead and utter his final judgment on every individual human being.

The phrase "my deare Monument" in line 78 may mislead the modern reader, for the husband's words would seem to refer to his wife's tomb or to a marble effigy of her. Yet at this time she has not yet been buried, for in the very next line the husband will order the grave closed (line 79). "Monument" here must then refer to the wife's dead body. It resembles a life-sized effigy of herself, as motionless and cold as a marble statue. (See *OED* 5c.) Shakespeare often uses the word to refer to a carved figure, an effigy.

With line 80 the grave is evidently now closed, for the husband describes the placing of the earth about his dead wife as a drawing of the bed curtains in the ancient ceremony of the bedding of the bride. The use of this metaphor to describe the placing of a young woman in the grave is a familiar one. It can be traced from the Middle Ages on down to A. E. Housman's "Bredon Hill." But it is here given a fresh application, for the bridegroom in this instance is not death, but the bereaved husband. Though the dead wife now lies in her bed to await the coming of the bridegroom, the final joining of bodies may be long postponed, for that must wait upon his own burial in her grave. Their final and absolute marriage will occur only when he "must / Marry my Body to that Dust / It so much loves" (lines 85–87).

With line 81 the husband begins his concluding address to his dead wife, the long farewell that closes the poem. She now once more becomes, in his imagination, a sentient being who can hear the promise that he makes to her as he speaks his "last Good-night" (line 83). He insists that some day he will return to "fill the roome / [His] heart keepes empty in [her] Tomb" (lines 87–88), for eventually he will be placed beside her in "that hollow Vale," the grave. The rest of the poem consists of his elaborations on this pledge.

Line 89 is the boldest in the whole poem. He implores (commands?) his wife to "Stay for mee there," as if the poor dead body could do anything else. Yet by putting matters as he has, he converts what, on the level of logic, is mere matter of fact into a solemn tryst. She is seen not as mere clay, however dear, but as a being to be conjured to keep the tryst. As for himself, the very facts indicating his own inevitable dissolution become proofs of his invincible determination to meet her at the elected trysting place. In fact, his passive waiting for his own end becomes, as he describes it in the poem, an active journey toward a sought-for goal.

Lines 92–114 are dominated by images of the journey, the husband's steady progress toward the death that shall bring the pair at last together. The journey is first treated as a sea voyage in which the bereaved husband sails steadily toward his "West / Of Life" (lines 98–99). As with a ship, his progress is indeed steady. The traveler does not have to stop at some wayside inn for a night's rest. Each morning when he wakes, he is truly eight hours closer to his goal than when he went to sleep. For even in sleep the body's process of dying goes on uninterruptedly.

The word *minute* in line 95—"Each Minute is a short Degree"—does double duty here: it carries a spatial as well as a temporal reference. For in calculating the longitude and latitude of a point on the globe of the earth, we measure distances in degrees and minutes. Sixty minutes make up a degree; three hundred sixty degrees, the full circle.

The word *bottome* in line 102 refers to the speaker's fancied vessel. (The word is still used in this sense today in maritime commerce.) Thus the husband voyages steadily westward "from the Sunne" (line 101) toward the realm of darkness and death. Having in mind the references to a sea voyage, most readers will assume that the "Compasse" mentioned in the next line is a mariner's compass, but if so, what can possibly be meant by "my Daye's Compasse downward beares" (line 102)? The magnetized needle of the compass swings horizontally on its axis; it cannot bear "downward."

Consultation of the *OED* clears up the mystery. "Compasse" here (*OED* 6) means "a circular arc, sweep, curve." One of the quotations illustrating this usage occurs in Captain Smith's *Seaman's Grammar* (1627): "Here doth begin the compass and bearing of the ship." The compass (arc) of the poet's imaginary ship is one following the curve of the globe. It is taking him below the horizon and on downward until it will reach his antipodes. Since the tide of life itself takes him toward death, the destination of all mortals, the bereaved man has no desire "to stemme [that] Tide" (line 103). Since it is carrying him toward his beloved wife, he welcomes it.

With line 105 the figure shifts from a journey by sea to a journey overland, the march of the rearguard of an army hastening to unite with the vanguard which has already joined battle with the enemy and gained a victory. Any Christian communicant of King's time, let alone a bishop, would remember Saint Paul's "O death where is thy sting? O grave where is thy victory?" To die in the Lord is to insure being admitted into eternal life—and for the devoted man and wife to be united.

It is this conviction that allows the speaker to tell his wife in the closing lines of the poem that he is content to wait upon his own "dissolution / With Hope and Comfort" (lines 116–17), though he feels obliged to ask her pardon for saying that he finds any comfort at all while still living apart from her.

Probably the most powerfully resonant lines in the poem are 111–14, those which recount the march of the rearguard to rejoin the now victorious vanguard. The speaker's own pulse becomes a drum to the beat of which his corpse marches on its way to join up with hers. His marches may be slow and take years to accomplish, yet nothing can stop him, he assures her.

> And, slowe howe're my Marches bee,
> I shall at last sitt downe by Thee.
> (lines 113–14)

So much for this brilliantly conceived and executed poem. Some years later, King wrote a poem entitled "The Anniverse," which, like "The Exequy," is an elegy on the death of Anne King. It begins with a tender address to the "Poore Earth, once by my Love inhabited." But after this sorrowfully affectionate opening it degenerates into a rather self-pitying whining over his own plight. Before the poem ends he even goes so far as to describe himself as bound alive to a corpse. This expression is downright grisly, and the realistic image of decay that it invokes is thoroughly self-serving: poor fellow, to be expected to have to endure this horror.

The failure of the poem requires no laboring. But taken as a biographical document it is interesting and may provoke the reader to wonder whether King was not, after six years, finding the widower's lot a truly unhappy one. One might even conjecture that it presages a second marriage.

Lawrence Mason, King's most thorough and conscientious biographer, believes that King did marry for the second time. He is properly very cautious on this subject. In fact he is plainly reluctant to accept the possibility that the author of "The Exequy" could possibly prove disloyal "to [Anne's] memory," or, much worse, "write about, woo [and] even win a second wife." But Mason as an honest scholar was forced by the weight of the evidence to conclude that King did make a second marriage. Since there is no record of a second marriage, the evidence has to be sought in King's poems.

One of them, of indeterminate date, is entitled "The Short Wooing." It is a rather perfunctorily witty proposal of marriage. The suitor does not wish a long probation. He wishes to hear the verdict at once. The lady addressed is reminded that she is the sole mistress of herself. The decision to accept or reject him is hers.

Since we cannot date the poem, the lady addressed might conceivably be Anne Berkeley herself. But if not, the poem would indeed suggest a second wooing. One notes that in any case it scarcely seems the utterance of an impassioned lover. But in itself the poem gives us little help with our question.

A second poem, also of indeterminate date, "The Legacy," is addressed to the speaker's wife. The content of the poem is a reasoned justification of second marriages. If he should die first, it is his wish that his widow will remarry. Among other things, he says

> Those were Barbarian Wives that did invent
> Weeping to Death at th' Husband's Moniment.
> (lines 49–50)

Was this poem perhaps addressed to his first wife, Anne? It might have been, since again we have no clue of the date of its composition. Or is the poem simply a speculative exercise? In any case, does it represent the bishop's true opinions about second marriages? If so, how do we square it with the implications of "The Exequy"? As for whether it expresses King's true feelings about second marriages, we can only guess. But we must remember that poems are not to be treated like sworn affidavits, presented in a court of law. Men do change their minds, and what was written during a period of racking grief does not necessarily represent the emotions of a later period.

Nevertheless, "The Legacy" would suggest that King was not of that monogamist cult of which Goldsmith's Vicar of Wakefield was a fanatic member. If we appeal to the historian, he will tell us that in the seventeenth century second and third marriages were frequent and even usual. One passage in "The Legacy," however, sticks in my mind.

> My Bodye's pamper'd care
> Hungry Corruption and the Worme will share,
>   That mouldring Relick which in Earth must ly
>   Would prove a guift of horrour to thine Ey.
>   (lines 15–18)

It recalls "If thou will bind mee Living to a Coarse" in "The Anniverse," a poem that was certainly written about his dead first wife, and it looks forward to a variation on this same gruesome image in our last piece of evidence, a poem entitled "St. Valentine's Day."

The particular lines I have in mind in that poem read as follows:

> Henceforth I need not make the dust my Shrine
> Nor search the Grave for my lost Valentine.
>   (lines 29–30)

In my opinion, "St. Valentine's Day" can be read only as a poem written by a widower who is proposing marriage to a prospective second wife: it simply makes no sense otherwise. The poem begins with a reference to one of the customs of Valentine's Day. As the *OED* describes it: "A person of the opposite sex [was] chosen, drawn by lot . . . as a sweetheart, lover, or special friend." The speaker of "St. Valentine's Day" tells the lady whom he addresses that he "could have wisht for your own sake / That Fortune had design'd a nobler stake / For you to draw" (lines 13–15). A few lines later he goes on to say, "Yet since you like your Chance" (line 19), and then in line 25, "Hail then my worthy Lot."

All this is spoken to the lady gallantly enough and with much self-deprecation. But there is certainly no passionate commitment, stated or implied. His future attachment to her has come about, so the poem would have it, by the workings of fate, and this theme of fatal action is reinforced by references elsewhere in the poem to his "cross Starres and inauspicious fate" which have for years "Doom'd [him] to linger here without [his] Mate" (lines 9–10).

The argument of the poem, if spelled out, amounts to this: Though I wish that Fortune had provided you with a "nobler stake" than I am, Fortune has been most kind to me in rescuing me from my residence in a tomb where I

> Like to a dedicated Taper lay
> Within a Tomb, and long burnt out in vain
> Since nothing there saw better by the flame.
> (lines 16–18)

This last figure has its own brilliance. It even reminds one a little of Donne, King's good friend, for whom King served as literary executor. A votive candle placed inside a tomb provides light, useless to the corpse within and not to be seen by anybody else.

The restiveness and unhappiness perhaps hinted at in "The Anniverse" would seem to have defined and realized itself in "St. Valentine's Day." The speaker of this poem, long bereaved, has resolved to give up living with his fruitless grief. There is a perceptible note of relief in the concluding lines that tell of his discovery that "I need not make the dust my Shrine / Nor search the Grave for my lost Valentine" (lines 29–30).

John Sparrow, who published an edition of King's poems in 1925, thought that the fact of a second marriage had been proved and referred to the closing line of "St. Valentine's Day" as an "ignoble sequel to 'The Exequy.'" Whatever the poem may or may not tell us about King's own life, it is on its own terms a sadly inept poem. For how can any lady welcome a lover who comes to her with hands confessedly grimy from scrabbling through the dust of his first love's grave?

Mason presents one more bit of evidence: an unsigned poem found in Harleian MS. 6917. Mason believed that it was written by King, and that the poem demonstrates that King was remarried by January 1, 1631. Margaret Crum, King's most recent editor (1965), argues that the author of this poem was not Henry King but his brother John. If so, what Mason interpreted as references to Henry's having a living wife in 1631 are incorrect. This bit of evidence for a second marriage thus collapses.

Crum's edition of King's poems has had the benefit of her discovery and the use of certain manuscripts not available to Mason and Sparrow. I judge that she is an excellent textual scholar, and I am grateful that in this essay I can quote from the texts of King's poems as she has established them. But in disproving Henry King's authorship of the poem in Harleian MS. 6917 she has not disposed of the possibility of a second marriage by King. What about the other poems: "The Anniverse," "The Legacy," "The Short Wooing"? Most of all, what about "St. Valentine's Day"? That strange poem is a veritable lion in the path.

Yet, interested as I am in biography and history, in this instance I am stalking bigger game. As I indicated earlier, I am interested in the bearing of historical fact on aesthetic judgment. Let us suppose that some scholar should come upon documentary evidence that Bishop King had remarried. Ought we in that case to think less of "The Exequy"?

My answer is that this magnificent poem stands above and apart from all the vicissitudes of King's personal life. I grant that the poem came out of his mind, a mind that was shaped by certain social and intellectual influences, and that if we want to enter fully into the poem we have to become acquainted with the language and culture that formed the mind of the man who formed the poem. But the umbilical cord connecting poem and poet has been severed. The poem now enjoys a life of its own, not to be affected by what subsequently happened to its author or what he caused to happen.

Let me be more specific still. Ought our appreciation and enjoyment of "The Exequy" to be affected by a subsequent reading of "St. Valentine's Day"? The latter poem and the related poem, "The Short Wooing," by the way, occur in only one manuscript, the Phillips MS. 9325. Suppose that this manuscript had never been discovered. What then? Would readers find "The Exequy" a more moving and sincere poem since they could never have read "St. Valentine's Day"? The hoped-for answer would be no—and not merely on the principle that what you don't know won't hurt you.

For me this negative answer does not depend upon an ignorance of the later poems, but on a more accurate sense of the nature of poetry and of the relation of poem to poet. Surely a good poem is not of such fragile structure that it can be destroyed or even damaged by our knowledge of later (or of earlier) events in the poet's own life. I have tried to show that "St. Valentine's Day" is an inept poem because of its own internal defects, and not because the poem shows that King could not live up to what some would say he had earlier pledged to do.

A truly good poem is not tarnished by the fact that its author wrote a bad poem or even two dozen of them, or even lived a bad life. For authentic poems are not inextricably attached to their authors so as to be affected by the authors' subsequent actions.

Many will, I hope, accept this as a reasonable view of the matter, but of those many, a good few will still cling to the concept of the poet's sincerity as a norm for evaluating his work. But the criticism of sincerity simply constitutes another way of tying the poem too closely to the poet.

In the first place, in real life sincerity is not easy to determine. In poets like King, about whom we know so little, it is almost impossible to determine, and such evidence as we have consists almost entirely of what we may glean from the very poems that are to be judged. Thus, let me repeat something said earlier, that the argument is hopelessly circular: we read the poem and find it truly moving, and so argue that it represents the author's sincere expression of his feelings. Then we proclaim that because the poet was sincere, his poem is tender and moving. In this way of putting matters, the term *sincere* becomes superfluous, and may be profitably discarded.

In their *Theory of Literature,* René Wellek and Austin Warren put the case against sincerity very well:

> There is no relation between "sincerity" and value as art. The volumes of agonizingly felt love poetry perpetrated by adolescents and the dreary (however fervently felt) religious verse which fills libraries, are sufficient proof of this. Byron's "Fare Thee Well . . ." is neither a worse nor a better poem because it dramatizes the poet's actual relations with his wife, nor "is it a pity," as Paul Elmer More thinks, that the MS shows no traces of the tears which, according to Thomas More's *Memoranda,* fell on it. The poem exists; the tears shed or unshed, the personal emotions, are gone and cannot be reconstructed, nor need they be.

Bishop King's dust was apparently never mingled in the same grave with Anne's, nor with that of any second wife, if there ever was such. Anne had been buried in London in 1624. Henry King died September 30, 1669, and as Bishop of Chichester was buried in his cathedral.

But what difference does it make? We have "The Exequy," and that poem is still very much alive. It is recoverable for any reader who will take the trouble to appropriate it for himself.

II

A Merry Bishop on the Death of Merry England

Richard Corbett

A PROPER NEW BALLAD INTITULED *The* FAERYES FARE-
WELL: *Or* GOD-A-MERCY WILL: *To be sung or whistled to the
Tune of the* Meddow Brow *by the Learned; by the vnLearned; To
the Tune of* FORTVNE

Farewell, Rewards & *Faeries,*
   Good Houswives now may say;
For now foule Slutts in Daries
   Doe fare as well as they;
And though they sweepe theyr Hearths no less   5
   Then Maydes were wont to doe,
Yet who of late for Cleaneliness
   Finds *sixe-pence* in her Shoe?

Lament, lament, old Abbies,
   The *Faries* lost Command: 10
They did but change Priests *Babies,*
   But some have changd your *land*;
And all your Children sprung from thence
   Are now growne *Puritanes*:
Who live as *Changelings* ever since   15
   For love of your Demaines.

At Morning & at Evening both
   You merry were & glad,
So little Care of Sleepe or Sloth
   These Prettie ladies had.   20
When *Tom* came home from labour,
   Or *Ciss* to Milking rose,

Then merrily, merrily went theyre Tabor,
　　And nimbly went theyre Toes.

Wittness those Rings & Roundelayes　　　　　　　25
　　Of theirs, which yet remaine,
Were footed in Queene *Maries* dayes
　　On many a Grassy Playne;
But, since of late *Elizabeth,*
　　And later *Iames,* came in,　　　　　　　　30
They never daunc'd on any heath
　　As *when the Time hath bin.*

By which wee note the *Faries*
　　Were of the old Profession;
Theyre Songs were *Ave Maryes,*　　　　　　　35
　　Theyre Daunces were *Procession.*
But now, alas, they all are dead,
　　Or gone beyond the Seas,
Or Farther for Religion fled,
　　Or elce they take theyre Ease.　　　　　　40

A Tell-tale in theyre Company
　　They never could endure,
And whoe so kept not secretly
　　Theyre Mirth, was punisht sure.
It was a iust & Christian Deed　　　　　　　45
　　To pinch such blacke & blew.
O, how the Common welth doth need
　　Such Justices as you!

Now they have left our Quarters
　　A *Register* they have,　　　　　　　　50
Who looketh to theyre Charters,
　　A Man both *Wise & Grave*;
An hundred of theyre merry Prancks
　　By one that I could name
Are kept in Store, conn twenty Thanks　　　　55
　　To *William* for the same.

I marvell who his Cloake would turne
　　When *Puck* had led him round,
Or where those Walking Fires would burne,
　　Where *Cureton* would be found;　　　　　60
How *Broker* would appeare to be,
　　For whom this Age doth mourne;
But that theyre Sp[i]ritts live in Thee,
　　In Thee, old *William Chourne.*

To *William Chourne* of Stafford Shire 65
    Give Laud & Prayses due,
Who every Meale can mend your Cheare
    With Tales both old & true.
To *William* all give Audience,
    And pray yee for his Noddle, 70
For all the *Faries* Evidence
    Were lost, if that were Addle.

This poem is one of the most charming of the minor poems of its era. The touch is light. If the poem hints at the passing of Merry England, the tone is not at all lugubrious. In fact, most readers apparently have found in it no more than a pleasant recounting of English fairy lore. Yet the poem makes, among other things, a commentary on affairs of church and state, and even a hint as to what was to come later. Most of all, it contains a shrewd insight into what was really at stake as a Royalist and churchman interpreted the issues.

To the casual reader even the title of the poem may be misleading. For the reader is likely to assume that the poem is a farewell uttered *by* the fairies, rather than a human being's farewell to the fairies—and a farewell to what else had been lost with their departure. Though the poem is quite well known to students of seventeenth-century poetry, it is now available to most readers only as an anthology piece. Only two editions of Corbett's poem have been issued since 1672.

The first stanza serves notice that the poem is something more than a gently nostalgic bit of reverie. The opening lines involve wit play. An obvious instance, of course, is Corbett's breaking down of the fossilized expression "farewell" into its two component parts and his restoration of each to independent life:

> For now foule Slutts in Daries
> Doe fare as well as they;
>   (lines 3–4)

There is also a play of wit in the phrase "good housewives." The *OED* indicates that, at the time Corbett wrote, *housewife* was frequently pronounced *hussy*—*housewife* having been reduced to *hussif* and that to *hussy*—and that the disparaging meanings now associated with *hussy* had already developed alongside the word's original neutral meaning. The *OED* concludes its comment on *housewife* with the following interesting note: "But many still [that is, in 1899] pronounce *huzwif, huzzie* . . . even when they write *housewife*."

Corbett, then, wrote in a period in which the same word could mean either *housekeeper* or *slattern*. Thus, the possibility of a play on the two meanings was open to him, and he evidently took advantage of it. For Corbett seems to be saying that now that the fairies have departed, the good hussy fares no better than does the other kind of hussy.

Corbett was not only a poet but also a churchman. Early in his life he entered holy orders and was to become eventually the dean of a cathedral and, later, a bishop. Thus, he was thoroughly conversant with the orthodox doctrine of rewards and punishments, and even in this poem he seems to be taking it into account. For he is careful to point out that the good housewives' zeal for cleanliness has in no way been lessened by the cessation of the fairies' rewards. Even though the fairies have departed, good housewives still sweep their hearths "no less / Then Maydes were wont to do" (lines 5–6). Good housewifery is doubtless its own reward; and yet the fairies' reward was welcome and life is now a bit more drab without it.

To perceive in this first stanza some hint of the Christian interpretation of rewards may seem overingenious. Yet Corbett's poem is, for all its playfulness, very much concerned—and quite seriously concerned—with what was happening to Christianity in England. The next five stanzas are full of that, and we shall miss the poem completely unless we are prepared to see just how seriously the poem engages the larger issues.

Unless we are willing to take such issues into account, it may seem particularly odd that, after consoling the good housewives on the departure of their friends the fairies, the poet should next extend his condolence to the abbeys. What reason have the abbeys to lament the departure of the fairies? Yet the poem does suggest that the dissolution of the abbeys was a part of a process in which the fairies too "lost Command."

Command over what, the reader may want to ask; and how is the preceding line related grammatically to "The *Faries* lost command"? The Folger MS. 452.4 reads "last command," as Professor Leslie Hotson once kindly called to my attention, along with other helpful notes on this poem.

To substitute *last* for *lost* at first seems tempting. Such a reading would simplify the grammar. Moreover, in view of what follows, the suggestion that the abbeys were the fairies' last British stronghold makes good sense. Yet *last* for *lost* will not do. Not only do the 1647 and the

1648 editions independently of each other read *lost,* but *command,* according to the *OED,* never meant *stronghold* or *redoubt.* Consequently, the meaning must be this: the abbeys ought to lament that the fairies lost command, and though what the fairies had command over is not specified, it must include the abbeys themselves.

At first glance this interpretation must seem preposterous, and all the more so in view of the line that immediately follows: "They [the fairies] did but change Priests' *Babies*" (line 11). For here the mischievous behavior that the folk attributed to the fairies is specifically related to the abbeys themselves. There may be even a suggestion that the fairies were trying to be helpful—to shield the abbeys from harmful gossip.

Corbett, by the way, was not the first to point out that the fairies had departed from England nor the first to comment on the fairies and priests' babies. Long before Corbett's time, Chaucer's Wife of Bath had had something to say about the departure of the fairies from England, and also about the sexual behavior of ecclesiastics. In King Arthur's day, she tells the other Canterbury pilgrims,

> The elf-queene with hir joly compagnye
> Daunced ful oft in many a greene mede.

She does so no longer, however, for the fairies have been driven out of the land by the prayers of the limitors and "othere holy freres," and so where an elf once walked, nowadays there walks the limitor himself. The Wife goes on to remark, with heavy sarcasm,

> Wommen may go now saufly up and down,
> There is noon other incubus but he
> And he ne wol doon hem but dishonour.

Unmarried women who gave birth to children, including those supposed to have been sired by priests, sometimes laid the blame on the incubus, an evil spirit who descended upon a woman in her sleep and had carnal intercourse with her. But the Wife of Bath intimates that she knows better: the real incubus is the limitor.

Whether or not Corbett knew the Wife's account, he has in his ballad made some alterations, such as the date of the fairies' departure and the reason for it. The fairies have fled from England much more recently—to be exact, in the third quarter of the sixteenth century—and apparently not because of the intrusion of Christianity. But no more than the

Wife does Corbett accuse the fairies of impregnating women. Moreover, Corbett has some special things to say about the "changes" that have occurred and about a new and special breed of changelings. The old folk belief had been that the fairies sometimes stole away a healthy newborn child and left a poor, thin deformed creature in its place.

In Corbett's ballad the origin of the changelings gets a very different account. The true origin is to be found in the dissolution of the abbeys and the acquisition of the Church lands. ("And all your Children sprung from thence [the taking from the abbeys of their lands] / Are now growne *Puritanes*" [lines 14–15].) In this new dispensation in which the abbeys have been dissolved and the fairies have fled, a truly awesome breed of authentic changelings has been produced.

Though the poet does not identify those who had divested the abbeys of their demesnes ("But some have changd your *Land*"), who could they have been other than Henry VIII, his ministers of state, and his favorites on whom the lands were bestowed? At all events, in spite of their reputation for mischievous conduct, the fairies cannot be blamed for the appearance of this new breed of changelings, who are not sickly and deformed in body, but whose deformation is within. In this instance at least, the fairies are clearly innocent, for, as the fourth and fifth stanzas of the poem will make plain, the fairies were not only friendly to the abbeys, but were themselves Roman Catholics. Little wonder that their expulsion from England was to be associated with the dissolution of the abbeys.

What the abbeys'—and England's—typical children were like before the drastic change is suggested in the third stanza, with its reminiscence of Tom, the farmboy, and Ciss, the milkmaid. Though the world which they inhabited was a merry one, the glimpse of it which Corbett's poem affords us is no mere pastoral scene of piping and dancing. It included work. It is a world neither of sheer drudgery nor of mere idleness.

> At Morning & at Evening both
>   You merry were & glad,
> So little Care of Sleepe or Sloth
>   These Prettie ladies had.
> When *Tom* came home from labour,
>   Or *Ciss* to Milking rose,
> Then merrily, merrily went theyre Tabor,
>   And nimbly went theyre Toes.

The fairies were often referred to as "the pretty ladies," and it is they who preside over the scene and presumably they who incite the merriment among the human beings who inhabit it.

To whom does "You" refer? Who are those who "merry were & glad"? Considerations of grammar and of the context point to "abbeys" as the reference. To be sure, Tom and Ciss were also evidently glad, as were, presumably, the other human beings of the world depicted, but as Corbett's poem makes clear, the fairies were this earlier world's animating spirit and enabling force. Even the abbeys were not gloomy and cheerless before the fairies lost command.

The century's great Puritan poet, John Milton, also had a glimpse of this merry world; at least in his youth he had it. His happy man in "L'Allegro" sees the village folk "Dancing in the Chequer'd shade . . . / On a sunshine Holyday" and, after night has fallen, drinking the "Spicy Nut-brown Ale" and entertaining themselves with stories about "Faery Mab" who would sometimes in the dairy help herself to curds and cream; about how sometimes they had been pinched by the fairies; about how the "*drudging Goblin*" earned the cream-bowl duly set out for him as his reward for threshing in the night more corn than ten day-laborers could have accomplished. Milton was obviously completely familiar with the fairy lore—as who in the period was not? The interesting matter in "L'Allegro" is his indulgent view of the very world that, as Corbett's poem will contend, Protestantism, and in particular its Puritanical manifestations, was in the process of destroying.

Are the abbeys being complimented by being called merry and glad, or are they being condemned? From the Puritan point of view, to call them places of merriment was an indictment. The usual Puritan case against them would be confirmed. On the other hand, the Roman Catholic party could hardly accept the abbeys' imputed character of merriment either, for their specific mission was spiritual and unworldly. What was Corbett's own attitude? Or more properly what is the attitude that one supposes he wished to convey in this poem? A final accounting will have to be postponed until we consider the rest of the poem. But one can say, even at this point, that the tone is not one of severe condemnation. The world over which the fairies presided and in which the abbeys existed is viewed with an indulgent eye. For the voice we hear in the poem is that of an Anglican high churchman. If he obviously dislikes what the Puritans would do, neither is he above teasing his Roman Catholic brothers.

It is not, however, until he reaches the fourth stanza that the poet provides evidence that the fairies were Roman Catholics. His first item is the fact that the departure of the fairies is to be dated from the death of Mary, the last Roman Catholic sovereign in England. The last fairy rings, he insists, were imprinted in her time. The poet's argument shamelessly depends upon the *post hoc, ergo propter hoc* fallacy. For how does he know that the fairy rings now visible were not made last night rather than some seventy-five years ago? The earlier dating rests solely on the poet's say-so. It is amusing to watch him in the next stanza brazen out his proof that the fairies are really Christians of the "old Profession."

The fairy rings that the poet says are still to be seen in his own diminished and less cheerful times are themselves worth a more particular comment. The fairies were believed to dance in a ring, and their dancing feet to print the grass, giving it a different hue from the grass within and without the circle. Various Elizabethan and Jacobean writers refer to these rings, including Shakespeare. In *The Tempest* (5.1) Ariel invokes, among other spirits,

> You demi-puppets, that
> By moonshine do the green-sour ringlets make
> Whereof the ewe not bites; and you, whose pastime
> Is to make midnight mushrumps.

I have seen fairy rings once or twice in the United States, though I was never told that they were made by the fairies. The scientists, of course, account for them with a much more prosaic explanation. They call them the product of certain fungi of the class *Basidiomycetes*. Curiously enough, Ariel's account of their origin is not much at variance with the scientific account. Ariel at least associates the elves or fairies who make the green-sour ringlets with those others who make another fungoid growth, the mushroom.

In using "roundelayes" to signify "rings," Corbett is taking liberties with the word. Fairy lore of the period is unanimous in insisting that the fairies danced in a ring, and it is true that the *OED* (3b) defines *roundelay* as "A fairy circle," but the only illustration of this meaning that it offers is this very line from Corbett's poem. Obviously, the poet has exercised his license as a poet in applying the term, naming the cause of an action to designate its effect.

Yet flimsy as is Corbett's argument for regarding the fairies as being Roman Catholics, his fifth stanza goes on to develop and enforce that association.

> Theyre Songs were *Ave Maryes,*
> Theyre Daunces were *Procession.*
> (lines 35–36)

Why does the poet, in this context, use the term *Procession?* Because it had in his day a distinctly liturgical association. Thus, the *OED* concludes its first definition with the following words: "marching along . . . , in a formal ceremonial way; esp. as a religious ceremony, or on a festive occasion," and in sense 3 defines the word as "A litany, form of prayer, or office said or sung in a religious procession." That the poet did have uppermost in mind the liturgical meaning is made certain by his writing "Procession" rather than "Processions." Moreover, "Procession" again points back to Roman Catholicism. At the Reformation all processions were abolished since they were associated with the Roman church and were particularly offensive to the Puritans.

The 1647 edition errs in making line 39 read "Or farther from Religion fled," for "from" misses the whole point. In Corbett's account the fairies were not pagans fleeing from Christianity. They were really recusant Roman Catholics fleeing to the Continent in order to maintain their faith. The poet is thus consistent in viewing the fairies as devoted members of "the old Profession."

Though the poet says that the fairies have "gone beyond the seas," the seas he had in mind were clearly not those of the North Atlantic. In the 1620s those who were fleeing to North America for the sake of their religion were Puritans. (Could it be significant that I have yet to see a fairy circle in Connecticut or Massachusetts? The fairies perhaps would not have expected a welcome in colonial New England.)

Line 37, which offers as one possibility that the fairies are "dead," must puzzle modern readers who automatically conclude that the fairies were immortal. But M. W. Latham, in *The Elizabethan Fairies,* points out that the popular conception held that a kind of symbiosis existed between the fairies and human beings. The fairies could help human beings as well as hurt them. But the fairies needed human help too—the cream bowl duly set out in Milton's "L'Allegro" is an instance. Latham puts matters emphatically: "The fairies of the sixteenth and seventeenth centuries required the beef and bread of mortals, and ate their way through the period, or, as James VI of Scotland stated, they 'eate and dranke, and did all other actions like naturall men and women.'"[1] Consequently, their death was a real possibility.

The modern reader is likely to regard Corbett's assumption that the fairies were Roman Catholic as a mere poetic whimsy, and perhaps it was. But Latham has shown that many people, including Bishop Samuel

1. M. W. Latham, *The Elizabethan Fairies: The Fairies of Folklore and the Fairies of Shakespeare,* 112.

Harsnet, George Chapman, Reginald Scott, James VI of Scotland, Edward Fairfax (in his *Discourse of Witchcraft*), and, of all people, Thomas Hobbes (in *The Leviathan*) believed that the fairies were papists.[2]

Keith Thomas, in his *Religion and the Decline of Magic,* quotes one, Goodwin Wharton, as asserting that the fairies "were Christians, serving . . . God that way, much in the manner of the Roman Catholics, believing [in] transubstantiation, and having a Pope who resides in England."[3]

If the fairies were by various authorities thought to be Roman Catholics, then that fact throws some light on lines 45–46 in the sixth stanza, where we are told that it was a "iust & Christian Deed" to pinch telltales "blacke & blew." The fairies were evidently entitled to claim that they were "Christian," though the poet, of course, may be using the term only mockingly. Whether Corbett himself really believed that the fairies were Roman Catholics is not the point. But, in the cultural context, his use of the term *Christian* was not a thoughtless slip of the pen.

Keith Thomas refers to "the Protestant myth that faery beliefs were an invention of the Catholic Middle Ages. . . . This much echoed view was grossly unfair. . . . But it was much employed by Protestant polemicists in the century after the Reformation and found its most attractive poetic expression in Bishop Corbett's 'The Faeryes Farewell.'"[4]

Corbett's is indeed the most attractive "poetic expression" of an assertion of such kinship. But why is it the most attractive? This is the kind of question any person concerned with poetry will want to ask.

My answer has already been implied, but I want to spell out some of its aspects. First, Corbett's treatment of the relationship is not essentially polemical. It presents the issues rather than arguing them. It dramatizes a situation rather than stating conclusions about it. The tone is playful and the mood genial. But he is far more sympathetic with the fairies and with Roman Catholicism than he is with Puritanism, though, in fact, he judges against both.

To my mind, Corbett's poem thus reflects rather accurately the Anglican *via media* as held by Anglicans such as Richard Hooker and later by Archbishop Laud. They take a middle ground, avoiding what was regarded as superstitious popery on the one hand and Puritan rigor on the other. In view of the unpretentiousness of "The Faeryes Farewell," such may seem a strong claim to make, and the poem, to be sure, does not

2. Ibid., 62–63.
3. Keith Thomas, *Religion and the Decline of Magic,* 611.
4. Ibid., 610.

assert any specific theological position. Yet the implications of the poem seem clear enough.

The dissolution of the monastic houses in the sixteenth century had been not so much a reformation of abuses as a looting expedition, carried out for political and mercenary purposes. The Anglican position would maintain that if the pre-Reformation church in England had its faults and excesses, its practice and piety were to be preferred to Puritan austerity and Puritan discountenancing of joy and beauty. Besides, the abuses of the pre-Reformation church could be corrected and, the Anglican would say, had largely been corrected in the Church of England.

The Anglican had no hankering after papistry, though he feared and detested an aggressive Puritanism. Anglicanism seemed to him to be a safe, reasonable, and attractive *via media*. This jolly man, the poet, who was to become a bishop, was not by temperament a Puritan, nor was he by doctrine, either. Nor was he, in spite of Puritan suspicions, a closet Roman Catholic. Like his ecclesiastical superior, Archbishop Laud, who was also falsely accused of being a secret Roman Catholic, Corbett believed that both extremes could be and ought to be avoided.

Consultation of William Haller's *The Rise of Puritanism* vindicates these assertions. Haller deals out an evenhanded justice to the Puritans, but he makes it plain that the Anglican position was reasonable and, within the limits of its time, quite tolerant. By contrast, it was the Puritans and the leaders of the Counter-Reformation who believed that they were forced to damn others. Corbett identifies the rise of Protestantism, particularly in its Puritan manifestations, with a materialism hostile to all poetry, whether that of the older church or that of England's peasant folklore.

What about Corbett the man and Anglican priest? Did he ever expect to hear his wife report that she had found a sixpence in her shoe? Or did he really ever hope to have a vision of

> Faerie Elves,
> Whose midnight Revels, by a forrest side,
> Or Fountain some belated Peasant sees,
> Or dreams he sees, while over head the Moon
> Sits Arbitress, and neerer to the Earth
> Wheels her pale course.
> (*Paradise Lost,* 2.781–86)

I think the answer is no. There are senses in which Corbett may be regarded as a "belated Peasant." His biographers frequently refer to a coarse and earthy streak within him. But peasant or not, I believe that Corbett was entirely too advanced historically to have had any doubt in deciding—had the vision ever occurred to him—that it could be anything more than an illusion, a dream. He had himself bade the fairies farewell long before he wrote his poem; but, in bidding them farewell, he had some knowledge of what he was giving up and what England had given up since "of late *Elizabeth,* / And later *Iames,* came in" (lines 29–30).

We must not suppose that Corbett's attitude here is special and peculiar. Robert Herrick, another Anglican poet-parson, in his masterpiece, "Corinna's Going a'Maying," shows a like easygoing accommodation of English quasi-pagan folk customs to Christianity. Thus, Corinna is advised to make her prayers brief on this special morning ("Few beads are best"). Moreover, it is expected that some couples will mate on the greensward ("Many a green-gown has been given; / Many a kisse"). But it is also expected that the happy couples will come in to have their marriages, already made according to the laws of nature, blessed by the Church ("chose their Priest").

It may be interesting to compare with view of a contemporary of a very different character with Corbett's notion that Protestantism, particularly in its Puritan manifestations, had finished off not only the abbeys but also the fairies and, with them, merry England itself. The celebrated John Selden, that learned and witty legal scholar, remarks in his *Table Talk* that "There never was a merry world since the fairies left dancing and the parson left conjuring." Both men link religion (at least that of the pre-Reformation church) with the English fairies, and Selden's "conjuring" parson seems to imply magical rites of some kind.

What did Selden mean by *conjuring*? Long before the seventeenth century the word had developed two quite diverse meanings. Definition 3 given by the *OED* reads "to constrain [a person to some action] . . . by appealing to something sacred; to charge or call upon in the name of some divine or sacred being; to adjure." Definition 7 reads: "To affect by invocation or incantation; to charm, bewitch. (By the Protestant Reformers applied opprobriously to consecration.)" As for the word *consecration*: Bishops were "consecrated" to that office (see *OED* 3), and the Puritans, Independents, and the Presbyterians wanted to do away with the order of bishops as unscriptural. Which of these meanings of *conjure* did Selden have in mind? Or did he quite deliberately choose to be ambiguous? Or did he mean to include something of both meanings?

The sentence in *Table Talk* that immediately follows Selden's comment on the dancing fairies and the conjuring parsons reads: "The opinions of the latter [the parson's] kept thieves in awe, and did as much good in a country as a justice of peace." This statement might seem to point to sense 3 of *conjuring:* that is, when the priest spoke with what purported to be divine authority, he put the evildoer in fear of divine retribution. And perhaps this is all that Selden meant. But a careful reader may have his doubts. The association of the fairies with such priestly "conjuring" hints that Selden felt that both the fairies' and the priest's power to punish involved superstitious awe. It is inconceivable that a man like Selden believed in the fairies, yet he knew that the countryfolk's belief in them may also have been good for society. Did Selden think of Christianity in a similar way? One commentator on Selden, Samuel H. Reynolds, goes so far as to say that though "Selden constantly professed a belief in a revealed religion [his recorded remarks on religion] are not at all what we should expect from a resolved serious Christian. They are rather in the language of one who takes religion under his wing, and finds it—like the virtue of humility—very good for other people."[5]

In any case, Selden's remark about the practical value of the priest's conjuring is pure Erastianism. To put such a view bluntly: the best reason to maintain the Church is that it is a powerful auxiliary to the constabulary. It serves to keep the populace out of mischief. Actually, both senses 3 and 7 are easily accommodated to the Erastian position.

Corbett was clearly no Erastian. Nor is there any reason to doubt that he was a true believer in the Christian faith, though he was not by temperament a particularly spiritual man. Certainly he was no John Donne or George Herbert, as his own poems testify. He was jolly and worldly and he could on occasion seem irreverent. John Aubrey records the following anecdote. Once, during the ceremony of confirmation, in which, as bishop, he was to lay his hands on the quite bald head of a man who had knelt before him, Corbett said to his chaplain who stood beside him, "A little dust, Lushington," as if he were trying to get a firm grip on a ball that he was to send rolling down a bowling alley. Christianity for Corbett was evidently a comfortable religion, not gloomy

5. Samuel Harvey Reynolds, ed., *The Table Talk of John Selden,* xxii.

and morose. He may have regarded his remark about this head that was as smooth as a bowling ball as implying a pleasant but serious metaphor. Thus, Corbett hoped to send this human soul rolling accurately on target to heaven.

Such an unseemly allusion would, of course, scandalize the Puritans. But then they were, in Corbett's opinion, bent upon making religion oversolemn and even upon eradicating the charm and joyousness from the life of the folk, and, far worse, they were bent on eliminating the beauty of holiness from the life of the Church.

As for "The Faeryes Farewell," if Corberrt believed that the Roman Church had acquired in the course of the centuries some superstitious beliefs and practices, that did not mean that he believed that the Roman Church was wholly corrupt or had gone completely astray. It had at least preserved the beauty of worship and a fundamental ecclesiastical order, both of which the Puritans threatened to sweep away. "The Distracted Puritan" in Corbett's poem of that name has gone mad "with zeale and godly knowledge." His constant refrain is

> Boldly I preach, hate a Crosse, hate a Surplice,
> 　　Miters, Copes, and Rotchets:
> Come heare mee pray nine times a day
> 　　And fill your heads with Crotchets.

When, however, the Puritans were not obviously mad and thus harmless, they were dangerous, and threatened the traditional life of the people and the orthodox and traditional religion of England, which for Corbett, as a good Anglican, was represented by the Church of England.

Though Corbett was a fun-loving man, his concerns engaged serious issues. The character of the Church and the rituals and liturgies through which it expressed the supernatural truths that it professed were therefore of paramount importance. He undoubtedly sensed the dangers to the whole culture presented by the Puritan cast of mind.

Yet Corbett could also be a good literary artist, and he is too good a poet here to make his farewell to the fairies seem portentous and oversolemn. After all, he has elected in this instance to write a ballad, a popular ballad that bears as its subtitle "Or God-a-Mercy Will" and is "to be sung or whistled to the Tune of the *Meddow Brow* by the Learned; by the unLearned; To the Tune of Fortune."

So, at the end of the sixth stanza, with its glance at the worsening state of affairs in England, "O, how the Common Welth doth need / Such

Justices as you [the fairies]" (lines 47–48), the poem completes itself in a series of exaggerated compliments to old William Chourne, the serving man of Corbett's future father-in-law, Leonard Hutten, who, like Corbett himself, was an Oxonian of Christ Church.

Now that the fairies have taken their departure, they have left in William Chourne their "*Register*" (the registrar of their acts and deeds). He it is that preserves their "Charters" (legal documents). In line 55, "conn twenty Thanks" means to "offer" thanks (*OED vb.* 4b).

The eighth stanza contains a number of puzzles. The first line can be translated as "I wonder" (marvell, *vb. OED* 1) who but for "Thee, old *William Chourne,*" would have known that one needed to turn his cloak inside out in order to break the fairy's spell after he had been turned about by Puck and so lost his way. (Corbett's poem "Iter Boreale" recounts how Corbett, Hutten, and two other Oxford friends, on their journey to Newark, had lost their way, and Chourne had urged them to remedy matters by turning their cloaks.)

The poet also asks who other than Chourne could have dealt with such phenomena as "Walking Fires" (the *ignis fatuus* or will-o'-the-wisp) and the raising up of the spirits of the dead. On "Cureton" and "Broker," Corbett's editors J. A. Bennett and H. R. Trevor-Roper supply the following note: "Presumably Staffordshire worthies whose spirits Chourne could conjure up. William Cureton was Rector of Synnerton, Staffs. in 1555."

Since Chourne was a Staffordshire man, the spirits he would wish to raise up would naturally be those of people of repute in his little world. These two local characters obviously were quite unknown to the great world outside. The 1647 edition of Corbett's *Poems* omits this stanza, perhaps because the manuscript text from which it derived lacked the stanza, but possibly simply because the editor couldn't make any sense of it. One of the manuscripts containing the poem, by the way, converts "Broker" into "Buckley"—which further suggests that the name of Broker was puzzlingly unfamiliar.

So it seems likely that in writing "The Faeryes Farewell" Corbett's principal object was the amusement of personal friends and Oxford associates. His "Iter Boreale" is filled with local and personal references. It is therefore rather surprising that "Iter Boreale" became quite popular. Bennett and Trevor-Roper supply a great many instances of seventeenth-century allusions to, or imitations of, it. "The Faeryes Farewell" apparently was even more popular in its own time, as the numerous manuscript copies of it show.

The poem comes to an end with further praise of "*William Chourne* of Staffordshire" and ends with a solicitation of prayers for "his Noddle."

> For all the *Faries* Evidence
> Were lost, if that were Addle.
> (lines 71–72)

Yet, even though the poem seems to trail off into a half-amused lauda-tion of the aged serving man's special fairy lore, the main thesis of the poem is nevertheless being quietly reinforced. The fairies *have* departed. The decisive proof is that future generations' very knowledge of them and their doings hangs by a thread—and may well perish with the memory of a single already aged man.

The reader, of course, does not have to take the poet's final prophecy seriously. Though Chourne's noddle has been addled for centuries, the memory of the English fairies has not been thereby lost. Yet the reader must not allow the obvious drollery of the ballad to conceal the poet's shrewd insight into the nature of the political-ecclesiastical forces so soon to come into violent conflict. Corbett's interpretation of the rela-tionship of Catholicism, Puritanism, and paganism can hardly be mere-ly whimsical.

On this matter one could wish for help and possible confirmation from the literary historian. But we know little of Corbett's life. There are two brief twentieth-century biographies, one by J. E. V. Crofts and one by Bennett and Trevor-Roper, printed as the introduction to their excellent edition of his poems. They write that Crofts's biographical essay is "full of . . . inaccuracies." They show themselves as being in-deed more careful and thorough historians than Crofts, and they are somewhat less sympathetic with Corbett. They emphasize Corbett's ambitious place-seeking and may well be right about it. They are proba-bly right also in stressing his indolence and laziness as a bishop.

Crofts's charmingly written essay is much more indulgent of Cor-bett's faults. Yet to my mind neither of these biographies fully succeeds in giving us the essential character of the man. Was he, as all three of them suspect, something of a cynic? What was the relation, if any, be-tween the merry scholar who made witty remarks and played practical jokes, and the high-church bishop? On this question neither the gossipy anecdotes that John Aubrey and Anthony à Wood pass on to us nor the formal records preserved among the State Papers provide an answer.

Yet do we not find a satisfactory answer in "The Faeryes Farewell"? In this poem Corbett skates on thin ice, it is true—though Swift, another Anglican parson, two generations later was to carry his "Tale of a Tub" over ice that was thinner still. But Corbett was no cynic. It ought to be thoroughly apparent, furthermore, that high churchman though he was, he was no Roman Catholic. And if he hated Puritanism, it was in part because he understood the Puritan better than the Puritan understood himself.

The attitude that Corbett takes toward religion in the poem is in fact rather sophisticated. It finds room for realism. It can accommodate a certain irony. It even allows for a good deal of tolerance. But I do not find it inconsistent with piety, though it would cause alarm to the superstitiously pious or to the grim and solemn precisionist of his own time or of ours.

III

Men of Blood and State

James Shirley

From *The Contention of Ajax and Ulysses,* 1659

The glories of our blood and state
  Are shadows, not substantial things;
There is no armour against fate;
  Death lays his icy hand on kings:
      Scepter and crown   5
      Must tumble down,
And in the dust be equal made
With the poor crooked scythe and spade.

Some men with swords may reap the field,
  And plant fresh laurels where they kill;   10
But their strong nerves at last must yield;
  They tame but one another still:
      Early or late
      They stoop to fate,
And must give up their murmuring breath,   15
When they, pale captives, creep to death.

The garlands wither on your brow,
  Then boast no more your mighty deeds;
Upon Death's purple altar now,
  See, where the victor-victim bleeds: 20
      Your heads must come
      To the cold tomb;
Only the actions of the just
Smell sweet, and blossom in their dust.

This well-known lyric has suffered the attrition often incurred by poems that are frequently anthologized. Too easy an acquaintance encourages us to take the theme and even the imagery for granted. We get the "moral" so easily that we often get little more than what we take to be that and the almost lilting rhythm and the steady thump of the rhymes.

The less attentive reader may not even get right the precise import of the poem. He may, for example, assume that the poem celebrates the common man and disparages those who boast of their noble blood, thus seeing the poem as a seventeenth-century anticipation of Robert Burns's "A Man's a Man for a' That." For doesn't the poem exalt the peasant's humble tools above the scepter of the king and the sword of the warrior?

Shirley does make use of these obvious symbols, but he uses his images to define a more specific meaning. In sum, the imagery is more than a vague allusion; it becomes part of the movement of thought and particularizes the meaning. Though the man who speaks the poem addresses members of the warrior class, there is no appeal to them to give up the shedding of blood nor any counsel to beat their swords into plowshares and their spears into pruning hooks. Instead, the poet does a bolder thing: he himself converts their weapons into such farming implements.

He begins his poem, however, by focusing attention on the warrior's defensive gear. Against Fate and Death his armor is too frail. Death penetrates it and lays his icy hands on the flesh of even a king; and his crown and scepter tumble down into the dust and so lie level with the peasant's "poor crooked scythe and spade."

The second stanza provides a poetic justification for that leveling. For like the peasant, the knight-at-arms sows and reaps the field. His harvest field is, of course, the battlefield, and his reaping tool is the sword. Moreover, the warrior, after his own fashion, plants. In overpowering his opponents, he sets growing "fresh laurels" with which to crown his victorious brow. Moreover, like the peasant, the conquering warrior serves another, working for the all-powerful reaper Death, who will some day mow down the warrior himself. In accomplishing this transformation, the poet does not force the "crooked scythe" into Death's skeleton hand. (He does not need to. The image of the grim reaper was quite as familiar to the seventeenth century as it is now to the twentieth. The poems by Aurelian Townshend and Francis Beaumont quoted below and in the next essay furnish thoroughly typical instances.)

Line 12, in the second stanza, makes the same point, but with a variation in the imagery. The warriors in their battle fury "tame but one another still." In due time Fate will tame them, and as "pale captives" they will not stride in triumph but "creep" their way to death.

The final stanza accomplishes the deflation of the warrior and the code by which he lives. The chaplets of victory woven from the fresh laurels planted at so much cost are bound to wither, for the victor, in the very process of winning, loses. The point is reinforced with another variation in the imagery. The victor who has laid his sacrificial victims on Death's bloody altar has not thereby appeased the implacable god but will find himself laid on the same altar.

In the concluding couplet, however, we are returned to the image of sowing and reaping. The only plants bearing "sweet blossoms" that grow out of the dust into which all mortal flesh crumbles are the "actions of the just."

At a hasty reading this concluding couplet may seem to be no more than a pious tag, rather clumsily hitched onto this stern rebuke to the warrior's pride. In fact, it is a proper development of the image that dominates the whole poem. As mere dust, lord and peasant are identical. Whether such dust will prove barren or yield flowers of immortality depends not upon rank and estate but upon whether one has acted justly.

Are we justified in using the phrase "flowers of immortality"? I think so, for such a meaning is implicit in a poem whose basic trope is that of sowing and reaping. One does not have to appeal to the fact that Shirley was originally in Anglican holy orders and later became a convert to Roman Catholicism, or that his readers were thoroughly versed in the Book of Common Prayer, replete with admonitions such as "Dust thou art, O Man, and unto dust shalt thou return," and in the King James Bible, with its solemn assertions such as "As thou sowest, so shalt thou reap."

As has been remarked earlier, this poem is clearly addressed to men of noble blood, men who have won their honors on the field of battle and are prepared to vindicate them there. The text of the poem should make this interpretation abundantly clear. But for readers who are left unconvinced by the internal evidence, plenty of external evidence is available.

The poem was first printed in 1659 in Shirley's *The Contention of Ajax and Ulysses for the Armour of Achilles*. This dramatic entertainment, as it was called, was, according to the title page, "nobly represented by young Gentlemen of Quality, at a private Entertainment of some person of Honour." (The public theater, closed by the Puritans, would not be reopened until after the Restoration of Charles II.)

Toward the end of the play, this poem was spoken or sung by the Greek seer Calchas as the corpse of Ajax was borne in by six of the Greek chieftains. Thus, the characters addressed in the play were men of noble blood, and for good measure, so were "the young Gentlemen of Quality" who acted their parts; and so, presumably, were those invited to the home of the "person of Honour."

As for "blood and state": by Shirley's time both words had acquired a number of meanings. As *state* is used in Shirley's poem, the *OED* (16b) defines it as "High rank, greatness, power," and its close association with rank and nobility is well established. For example, the *OED* (26) indicates that, in appropriate contexts, *state* referred to "the rulers, nobles, or great men of a nation" themselves.

In the context of this poem *blood* carries two quite different, though closely related, meanings. Men of "blood" are men of breeding—of proper lineage and recognized bloodlines. But "blood" is also the liquid that courses through human arteries and veins and that may be shed in combat. In earlier times the man-at-arms was typically a man of blood in both senses. In battle he spilled the blood of his enemies and often suffered some loss of his own. The reference to the "purple altar" where the victor-victim bleeds obviously puts a heavy stress on this second sense.

As for the first sense: originally, a place among the nobility was achieved through one's prowess as a fighting man. The knight and baron served the king in this way, and originally the king himself was a fighting man. By the time of the later Tudors and the Stuarts, such was, of course, no longer true. Henry VII was probably the last English king who might have been reckoned a force in combat. In the Battle of Bosworth in the late sixteenth century Henry fought it out with Richard III for the crown. But even in Shirley's day many young nobles still fought and died in battle: witness the English Civil War. In any event, the tradition, reinforced by heraldry, chronicle, and poetry, was still very much alive.

The nobility and the county gentry were also still closely identified with the land, and thereby with the whole process of sowing and reaping. If their landed estates were mismanaged or if nature was unpropitious, they soon suffered the consequences. Granted that they did not literally wield the crooked scythe, they knew what it was and recognized its ultimate importance.

A rather charming poem of the period makes this point about the relation of the landed class to their estates. It is by Richard Fanshawe.

His subject is Charles I's 1630 proclamation "Commanding the Gentry to reside upon their Estates in the Country." Though the whole continent of Europe seems embroiled in wars, the king has kept England at peace and now bids the "Landed Heyres" to enjoy that peace—at their homes on their own lands.

> Nor let the Gentry grudge to goe
> Into those places where they grew
> But thinke them blest they may doe so.

The poet also urges their ladies to give up "The smoky glory of the Towne," addressing them directly in the closing stanzas.

> Beleeve me Ladies you will finde
> In that sweet life, more solid joyes,
> More true contentment to the minde,
>   Than all Towne-toyes. . . .
>
> Plant Trees you may, and see them shoote
> Vp with your children, to be serv'd
> To your cleane boards, and the fair'st Fruite
>   To be preserv'd:
>
> And learne to use their severall gummes,
> "'Tis innocence in the sweet blood
> "Of Cherryes, Apricocks, and Plummes
>   "To be imbrue'd."

Even in this poem *blood* appears. Although it is used figuratively, it carries hints of the double sense in which Shirley uses it in his lyric. For the blood that will stain the hands of these wellborn ladies will be, as befits their sex, wholly innocent: the juice of their homegrown fruits.

In sum, for Shirley's special audience, sowing and reaping, far from being archaisms, as they probably are for city-bred readers of our day, were totally familiar, not only through his readers' literature and religion, but from the daily life that went on all around them.

One notes that Shirley's poem makes no mention of the middle classes, and in a brief song addressed to seventeenth-century gentlefolk this is not surprising. Fanshawe's poem does so, but only briefly and in disparaging terms. By leaving London one can avoid the "griping Scrivners hand," the more "byting Mercers hooks," and the "bayt of oyled hands / And painted looks." Evidently, for such people as Fanshawe (and perhaps for Shirley also), all that really counted for the good estate of the realm were the nobility, the gentry, and those who worked their lands.

Ironically, the growing London middle class was to prove to be a powerful revolutionary force in the very next decade. In saying this, one does not forget that many of those who took the side of Parliament were of the nobility and the gentry. Oliver Cromwell himself was a country gentleman. Nevertheless, the poems of Royalists like Fanshawe were a sign of the times—of the Court party's failure to see that the world of the landed gentry and their tenants was no longer all that counted in England.

We do not know how long Shirley's song had been composed prior to its publication in *The Contention,* which was printed in 1659. *The Oxford Companion of English Literature* down to its fourth edition in 1967 describes it as "'the fine song which old Bowman used to sing to King Charles' and which is said to have terrified Cromwell." Such association of King Charles with Cromwell suggests that the king was Charles I. That "The Glories of Our Blood and State" pleased Charles and terrified his great opponent provides a piquant irony.

It is a shame to spoil so good a story, but the king could not have been Charles I. *The Oxford Companion* cites no authority for its comment, but the source on which it relied was probably a note that the antiquary William Oldys wrote in the margin of his copy of Gerard Langbaine's *Account of the British Dramatick Poets,* now in the British Library. Oldys wrote:

> In this *Contention* is the fine Song which old Bowman used to sing to King Charles, and which he has often sung to me—The Glories of our Birth [*sic*] and State &c and therein also are the fine lines
>
>> Your Heads must come
>> To the cold Tomb
>> Only the Actions of the Just
>> Smell sweet, and blossom in the Dust.

Since Oldys was not born until 1698, old Bowman must have been old indeed if he could have sung the song to Oldys and also to Charles I, who died in 1649.

Dr. Harriet Harvey Wood has kindly examined this volume for me and finds in it no reference to Cromwell whatsoever; nor is there any in the three other annotated copies of Langbaine that the British Library possesses. But she reports that in the interleaved copy that once belonged to Joseph Haslewood and in which the annotations of Oldys and other antiquaries are copied, the following note on Shirley's song occurs: "Probably Bowman the Actor above mentioned."

This conjecture is surely right. John Bowman (or Boman, ?1651–1739) was a well-known actor and singer of the time. He is said to have had a fine bass voice. In 1675 he became a member of the King's Musick and apparently knew Charles II well. From *A Biographical Dictionary of Actors, Actresses . . . and Other Stage Personalities in London, 1660–1680,* we also learn that Bowman "often shared a bottle with Charles II" and once attended "a party at Nell Gwyn's house in Pall Mall where [he] and others provided entertainment for Nell, Charles, the Duke of York and others." So he did sing for Charles II, and Oldys is probably correct in specifying "The Glories of Our Blood" as one of the songs. One had not guessed that the Merry Monarch possessed so catholic a taste.

The fifth edition of *The Oxford Companion* edited by Margaret Drabble (1985) makes the proper correction, with the terse statement that "The glories of our blood and state" was "a favourite with Charles II." But I have allowed my own account of the matter, written some several years ago, to stand. For the reader may be interested in how it was determined that the monarch referred to was the second Charles, not the first. In any case, a more detailed account seems proper in a book that attempts to marshal for each poem discussed all the relevant extrinsic evidence.

The theme of death as the leveler who refuses to spare the king himself was, of course, an ancient and familiar one. The poets often used it, and particularly the dramatic poets of the century. Several instances from Shakespeare at once come to mind, notably such passages as this:

> for within the hollow crown
> That rounds the mortal temples of a king,
> Keeps Death his court.
>
> (Richard II, 3.2)

Francis Beaumont's poem "On the Tombs in Westminster Abbey" will provide another typical instance. The quotation from it that follows begins with line 23 of the poem.

> Here's an acre sown indeed
> With the richest royalest seed,
> That the earth did e'er suck in

25

Since the first man died for sin.
Here the bones of birth have cried,
"Though Gods they were, as men they died."
Here are sands (ignoble things)
Dropped from the ruined sides of kings,   30
With whom the poor man's earth being shown
The difference is not easily known.
Here's a world of pomp and state,
Forgotten, dead, disconsolate;
Think, then, this scythe that mows down kings   35
Exempts no meaner mortal things.
Then bid the wanton lady tread
Amid these mazes of the dead;
And these truly understood
More shall cool and quench the blood   40
Than her many sports aday,
And her nightly wanton play.
Bid her paint till day of doom,
To this favor she must come.
Bid the merchant gather wealth,   45
The usurer exact by stealth,
The proud man beat it from his thought,
Yet to this shape all must be brought.

This is in many respects a fine poem and contains truly arresting lines, such as "Mortality, behold and fear / What a change of flesh is here!" and "Here are sands (ignoble things) / Dropped from the ruined sides of kings." The poem is more declamatory than Shirley's and more flatly moralistic. By contrast, Shirley's poem is notable for its economy of images—images through which the theme is developed.

Unlike Shirley's poem, Beaumont's is addressed, not to the nobility, but to a very general audience, indeed to all of less than royal rank. His poem is a kind of a fortiori argument: if death can so completely conquer the highest and mightiest of mortals, clearly it can do so to all lesser folk. As in Shirley's poem, Death is here a mower, his instrument the scythe. But Shirley has managed his use of this conventional figure much more dexterously than has Beaumont.

The great weakness of Beaumont's poem, however, is its conclusion. The "wanton lady" gets rather more than her due of attention and castigation. The merchant, the usurer, and the proud man are reminded of the "shape [to which they] all must be brought." At this rate, the poet could go on and on with further examples until he has simply wearied himself out and wearied out his reader.

Such development as there is in the poem comes to a conclusion with "Think, then, this scythe that mows down kings / Exempts no meaner mortal things." These lines provide a crisp summary of the one theme that has dominated the poem. In its control of imagery and tone, and in its achieved unity, then, Shirley's poem carries off the honors.

It is interesting and may be profitable to compare Shirley's poem with a poem of related theme written in the next century: Thomas Gray's "Elegy Written in a Country Churchyard." Neither poem, one observes, carries any revolutionary import. Shirley's song reminds the gentry and the nobility that death is no respecter of persons and will in the end level them with the husbandman. Though this song is clearly addressed to the nobility, they are not rebuked for their possession of power or for the fact that they are "men of blood." They are simply reminded that they are nonetheless mortal. So it is with Gray's "Elegy." The speaker in the poem accepts the social conditions that exist, but he does take note of the waste of potential talents—of poets like Milton, whose humble lot condemned them to remain mute; of potential statesmen who, given happier opportunities, "the rod of empire might have swayed."

Yet the elegist discerns positive advantages in the humble lot of these villagers buried in the churchyard. Though fate has denied them the opportunity to win fame and power, they have been protected from the temptations that always attend power. As the elegist puts it, though their "lot circumscribed" their "growing virtues," it also confined their powers to commit crimes. Gray presumably would have heartily endorsed Lord Acton's dictum that "power tends to corrupt; absolute power corrupts completely."

In fact, Gray's "Elegy" reveals an underlying suspicion of power and high degree that is quite absent from "The Glories of Our Blood and State." Though Gray is not cynical, yet he shows no faith in natural man—in what in our day has been called the common man. Given the means and the opportunity, his "village Hampden" might well have become a "Cromwell [guilty] of his country's blood." The assumption is that the motive is nearly always there.

The meditation on the humble graves of the villagers under the open sky and the sumptuous tombs of the great under the roof of some great abbey church leads to the elegist's choice of a burial place for himself. Though his own lot did not rule out all hopes that he might have won a more glorious tomb, he chooses a grave in the churchyard.

Yet we must not misconceive his motive. It is not a democratic impulse or a sentimental identification with the simple village folk. Rather, he has come to see the final vanity of all worldly ambition and chooses instead a life of meditation and contemplation. In the epitaph he has composed for himself, he indicates to the chance passerby that "Melancholy mark'd him for her own." This eighteenth-century Penseroso deliberately chooses the contemplative life over the active life. Not only does he find it richer and more satisfying to the spirit. His meditations have revealed the hollowness of glory. "Vanity of vanities, all is vanity." The goddess that had claimed him is Milton's

> Goddess sage and holy
> . . . divinest Melancholy
> Whose Saintly visage is too bright
> To hit the Sense of human sight;
> And therefore to our weaker view
> Ore laid with black staid Wisdom's hue.

Is the elegist's choice, then, that of the Christian ascetic? Perhaps, but I should think that the influence of classical philosophy is even more powerfully manifest here. I sense more of the Stoic view of the relation of man to nature than I do of the doctrine of Original Sin. To be sure, the epitaph is formally an expression of Christian humility and hope, but the God to whom the appeal is made is far more remote than the God of Herbert and Donne.

Though his song is too short to provide more than meager evidence of Shirley's Christianity, it does indicate one important aspect of it. His Christianity has not been touched by the doctrine of justification by faith alone, the doctrine so much stressed by the Puritans. The concluding couplet of Shirley's song, "Only the actions of the just / Smell sweet, and blossom in their dust," is as orthodox and as medieval as the conclusion of the popular fifteenth-century morality play *Everyman*. When Everyman is summoned by Death, he is deserted by his friends such as Fellowship, Kindred, Knowledge, Goods, Beauty, and Strength. Only Good Deeds promises to keep him company through death itself. Such is what one would expect of a man who took orders in the Church of England and later converted to Roman Catholicism.

Thomas Hardy salutes the English plowman, but not as he "homeward plods his weary way." In "In Time of 'The Breaking of Nations'" he is

> Only a man harrowing clods
> In a slow silent walk

With an old horse that stumbles and nods
Half asleep as they stalk.

Only this smoke without flame
From the heaps of couch-grass
Yet this will go onward the same
Though Dynasties pass.

Yonder a maid and her wight
Come whispering by;
War's annals will cloud into night
Ere their story die.

The contrast between the peasant and the man of power is again very much alive in this little poem, but the men of power are only implied by the title of the poem and in the reference to passing "Dynasties."

Hardy provides a footnote reference for the title: "Jeremiah 51:20." In the verse cited, Jehovah addresses Israel, saying, "Thou art my battle-axe and weapons of war; for with thee will I break in pieces the nations, and with thee will I destroy kingdoms." But plainly all that Hardy owes to the cited verse is the resonant phrase "In the Time of 'The Breaking of Nations.'" (The poem is dated 1915.) Hardy's poem is not addressed to Israel but to whoever has ears to hear; and in the poem Jehovah has no place at all.

The poem concerns itself only with what is lasting and essential in the life of mankind, with fertility in its two needful forms: the production of food and the continued reproduction of mankind. Besides these two activities, all else—so the poem implies—is trivial. Which army will win victory or which dynasty will gain power is unimportant. Food for the body and new young bodies to be nourished—these are essential if mankind is to endure. War and dynastic glory are ultimately irrelevant to the human enterprise. The old man preparing the field for planting and the youth and maiden plighting their troth are things that must go on as long as this globe is to be inhabited by human beings.

Hardy, as we know, was, as a man and as an English citizen, very much committed to Britain's war effort. He wrote a good many patriotic poems during this period. But in this one he takes the long, long view in which everything except the survival of mankind blurs out. God, patriotism, progress, and a host of other concepts and values are simply ignored.

It is a poem that could hardly have been written in the seventeenth century or even in the eighteenth. It reflects a different intellectual climate. The point is so obvious as to be hardly worth the making. But that is not the point I mean to stress here. No one has ever doubted that poems (and novels and plays) are products of the culture out of which they came, and consequently at some level they must reflect that culture. But that fact does not prevent our assessing these literary documents on other levels, including what they can tell us about ourselves and about the universal human condition. Moreover, if we want to make comparative studies, a concern for the structure of a literary work and its details and even the nuances of its meaning may actually promote such study. For often the detail and nuances of a work reveal the special nature of its cultural matrix.

IV

A Court Poet

Aurelian Townshend

Aurelian Townshend's work is little known today. Many years ago, in reviewing Grierson's *Oxford Book of Seventeenth Century Verse,* T. S. Eliot referred to the "pleasing tinkle" of Townshend's verse. The phrase has a point: Townshend does not pretend to profundity, and his modesty on this point is thoroughly justified. Yet one can learn a good deal about the style of a period from the work of its poetasters. The best of Townshend will throw its tiny beam of illumination on the characteristic virtues and deficiencies of the English poets of the first half of the century. One of his best poems, "To the Countess of Salisbury," will illustrate.

> Victorious beauty, though your eyes
>   Are able to subdue an hoast,
>   And therefore are unlike to boast
> The taking of a little prize,
> Do not a single heart dispise.
>
> It came alone, but yet so arm'd
>   With former love, I durst have sworne
>   That where a privy coat was worne,
> With characters of beauty charm'd
> Thereby it might have scapt unharm'd
>
> But neither steele nor stony breast
>   Are proofe against those lookes of thine,
>   Nor can a Beauty lesse divine
> Of any heart be long possest,
> Where thou pretend'st an interest.
>
> Thy Conquest in regard of me
>   Alasse is small, but in respect
>   Of her that did my Love protect,

Were it divulged, deserv'd to be
Recorded for a Victory.

And such a one, as some that view
  Her lovely face perhaps may say,
  Though you have stolen my heart away,
If all your servants prove not true,
May steale a heart or two from you.

Townshend's editor, Sir E. K. Chambers, thinks that the countess addressed was Catherine Howard, daughter of Thomas, earl of Suffolk. On December 1, 1608, she had married William Cecil, the second earl of Salisbury. John Donne addressed one of his verse letters to her. It is not one of his successes. It pays the lady high compliments in a rather ponderous style. Donne proclaims the countess to be "Faire, great, and good," and then, through some eighty and more lines and with much finespun argument, sets out to justify his use of such powerfully complimentary adjectives.

Extravagant laudation was, of course, the order of the day. When the person ascribed or addressed was a noble lady, it was de rigeur. Donne's method for giving a measure of credibility to his praise is to justify it logically—or at least through a show of logic. Townshend's strategy is quite different. Though the courtier who speaks the poem declares the countess to be first in his heart, nearly all the rhetorical energies of the poem are devoted to praising the charming attractions of his former love. So the poem has to be deemed either inept to the point of awkwardness, or else almost a naughty teasing. It is certainly not straightforward flattery.

In the first stanza, the courtier does salute the countess as a "Victorious beauty," victorious not only over him but over so many others that she might well dismiss this latest conquest as having yielded only "a little prize," one scarcely worth the taking. In the next three stanzas the courtier undertakes to offer the countess reasons for considering her conquest of his heart to be, after all, of some account.

With a proper self-depreciation he concedes that in intrinsic worth he is indeed paltry. What gives some consequence to her conquest of him is the strength of the resistance that her beauty had to overcome. Up to this point he had believed that he was fortified against the arrows of any new love, for he was dressed in a "privy coat"—a coat of mail worn beneath one's outward garb. But even this missile-proof vest, "With characters of beauty charm'd," was unable to deflect the darts that emanated from the countess's eyes. Neither magic spell, "steele nor stony breast," he declares, "Are proofe against those lookes of thine." Such power is truly invincible. Thus, if the lady will take into account the strength of his allegiance to his former love, her conquest of him can fairly "be / Recorded for a Victory."

Rationally, the "Victorious beauty" can scarcely object to what has been said. But it must seem somewhat odd, even rather disconcerting, to learn that this admirer who declares himself so absolutely hers seems unable to get out of his head the charms of his sometime mistress.

Worse is to come. In the final stanza, the rather ambiguous praise of the countess's beauty becomes downright teasing, and the courtier's former loved one is brought into even sharper focus. Her "lovely face" may very well cause observers—perhaps impartial witnesses?—to remark that "Though you have stolen my heart away," her loveliness is such that she "May steale a heart or two from you."

The whole game of extravagant compliment and high-flown declarations of love is recognized to be just that, a game, in which even a victorious beauty may occasionally lose. Small wonder that in one of the manuscripts in which this poem occurs, it is entitled "A Warning." The lady must not become overconfident of her powers.

Assuming that the countess of Salisbury read this poem, what did she think of it? Did she frown or did she turn away with a hearty laugh? We have, of course, no way of knowing.

Sir E. K. Chambers was apparently aware of the anomalous character of a compliment that turns into an admonition. He points out Townshend's connection with the House of Cecil and suggests that it was perhaps Townshend's intimacy with the family that allowed him to address the countess in these mischievous verses. Most such court flattery of the period lacks the sense of reality that is here invoked by the poet's use of humor and the salt of wit.

Wit and a modest self-depreciation are to be found in another bit of Townshend's *vers de société*, "Youth and Beauty," and because they are present, redeem this poem also from being merely fluff.

> Thou art so fair, and yong withall,
>   Thou kindl'st yong desires in me,
> Restoring life to leaves that fall,
>   And sight to Eyes that hardly see
>   Halfe those fresh Beauties bloom in thee.   5
>
> Those, under sev'rall Hearbs and Flowr's
>   Disguis'd, were all *Medea* gave,
> When she recal'd Times flying howrs,

And aged *Aeson* from his grave,
   For Beauty can both kill and save.   10

Youth it enflames, but age it cheers,
   I would go back, but not return
To twenty but to twice those yeers;
   Not blaze, but ever constant burn,
   For fear my Cradle prove my Urn.   15

We cannot date the poem, but line 13 would suggest that Townshend was by this time past forty. Whatever the speaker's age, he is obviously much older than the young girl to whom the poem is addressed. Her youthful beauty, he tells her, kindles "yong desires" in him. Yet he is in the autumn of his life, and his age-dimmed eyes are able to see hardly half the "fresh Beauties" of springtime that bloom in her. Such beauties, he declares, were in fact the effective ingredients that the enchantress Medea used in restoring youth to her aging father-in-law, Aeson. We are told that Medea put into her youth-restoring pot "Hearbs and Flowr's," but these were only the outward forms of the true wonder-working power: the beauty of a young woman in her springtime. Such would seem to be the implication of "Those [beauties of yours] under sev'rall Hearbs and Flowr's / Disguised, were all *Medea* gave." *Under* here denotes "that a thing is presented in a certain form or aspect" (*OED* 16). Thus, for instance, in the Eucharist, Christ's body and blood are received "under" the forms of bread and wine.

When the daughters of Aeson's half-brother Pelias asked Medea to perform the same service for their father, she pretended to comply. She filled a cauldron with water into which she put herbs and flowers. She killed and dismembered an old ram and placed the pieces in the cauldron. Soon a young lamb jumped out. With this proof of her skill, she persuaded Pelias's daughters to kill their father, cut him up, and put him in the pot. But Medea had left out the wonder-working ingredients. Nothing came out. Thus she revenged her husband upon his usurping uncle.

The man who speaks the poem is, of course, far from imputing malicious motives to this young beauty. Nevertheless, her beauty, like all beauty, is a potent force: "it can both kill and save." Old men must be cautious of its blinding rays. He describes its normal and proper role by saying, "Youth [beauty] inflames, but age it cheers."

Therefore, he does not seek restoration to the youthful ardors of twenty that her beauty might well set ablaze, but is content to remain a comfortable forty or so, and simply to enjoy beauty's comforting warmth. He sums up the whole matter very prettily in the last two lines:

> Not blaze, but ever constant burn,
> For fear my Cradle prove my Urn.

Yet if he shrinks from being set blazing, he can at least promise that his glow will be "constant." His admiration of her will endure, not go out in a flash of fire, as inconstant youthful love so often does. But his caution is frankly realistic and self-regarding. He knows that he is no longer up to the high ardors of youth: a great gust of passion might well carry him off.

The concluding line quite clearly glances back to the Medea reference: her enchanted pot which promised to be the cradle for Pelias's new infancy in fact turned out to be the receptacle of his dead body. In the seventeenth century, when Townshend's readers were steeped in the classics, such references as that to the Medea story would have been picked up immediately, and not have had to be tediously spelled out. The little poem, then, for its proper audience, is deft and light-fingered, not labored. What one would call special attention to is its handling of tone. It is much more than the usual piece of rather empty flattery. The opening is rather tender: "Thou art so fair, and yong." Part of the girl's charm for the older man evidently is that she is not at all aware of her power. She is indeed no Medea. She is not even the conscious beauty, taking pride in herself.

In writing for a select audience, the poet of this period had a great advantage. His readers had received basically the same general education, were familiar with the same literary conventions, and shared the same basic beliefs. Such a literary situation, however, has its own limitations. There is the ever-present danger of falling into a monotonous and conventional handling of the old materials and rhetorical devices, or else, in an effort for novelty, torturing them into distorted and extravagant forms. The poetry of Abraham Cowley will provide obvious examples of this latter danger.

Townshend's "A Dialogue betwixt Time and a Pilgrime" again shows the poet taking skillful advantage of his readers' acquaintance with a stock of familiar allusions and poetic conventions. He succeeds in achieving concision without sacrificing intensity.

> *Pilgr.*   Aged man, that mowes these fields.
> *Time.*   Pilgrime speak, what is thy will?
> *Pilgr.*   Whose soile is this that such sweet Pasture yields?

                    Or who art thou whose Foot stand never still?
                        Or where am I? *Time.* In love. *Pilgr.* His   5
                    Lordship lies above.
    Time. Yes and below, and round about
                        Where in all sorts of flow'rs are growing
                    Which as the early Spring puts out,
                        Time fals as fast a mowing.   10
    Pilgr. If thou art Time, these Flow'rs have lives,
                        And then I fear,
                    Under some Lilly she I love
                        May now be growing there.
    Time. And in some Thistle or some spyre of grasse,   15
                    My syth thy stalk before hers come may passe.
    Pilgr. Wilt thou provide it may. *Time.* No. *Pilgr.* Alleage
                        the cause.
    Time. Because Time cannot alter but obey Fates laws.
    Cho. Then happy those whom Fate, that is the stronger,   20
                    Together twists their threads, & yet draws hers the
                        longer.

The poem begins with an unidentified Pilgrim making his way to an
as yet unspecified shrine or other goal. Yet the seventeenth-century
reader would have had no difficulty in accepting the situation implied.
The poetry of the day is filled with pilgrims, often on figurative pil-
grimages, and the goal toward which they traveled is not necessarily the
shrine of some saint, but the breast of a loved one. Moreover, in the
sermons and homilies then current, the pilgrimage takes an even more
generally symbolic form: every man was conceived to be a pilgrim, a
wayfarer moving toward salvation or damnation.

As for the aged man with the scythe, even if the title of the poem did
not identify him as Time, the fact that his scythe never stands still would
tell the reader who this strange husbandman was. The cartoonists and
illustrators of our present day still depict Time so, particularly when
they need a symbol for the waning year.

The Pilgrim himself, being a character within the poem and thus
lacking the reader's acquaintance with its title, naturally takes a little
longer to discover the harvester's true identity. At first, he seems to
regard the aged man as simply another human being, and his first question is to inquire who is the owner of a field so fertile. (The quantity of
flowers makes its fertility abundantly evident.) But without waiting for
an answer, the Pilgrim goes on to ask two other questions: who is this
mower and in what location does the questioner himself now stand?

These questions tumble forth rather confusedly, as from a person who may have begun to realize that there is something strange about the whole scene. Yet when the aged man chooses to answer the pilgrim's third question ("Where am I"?) by saying "In love," the pilgrim readily accepts the unexpected specification of a mental state rather than a physical one. The reader has a right to assume this, for the Pilgrim immediately shifts his inquiry into the new context. He asks how Eros, a transcendent god, can exercise his lordship in this world below. The aged man agrees as to Love's transcendence, but points out that the love god's lordship also lies "below, and round about," as witness the flowers that he has caused to grow here. The love god is then not merely the god of ideal love, but also the god of fertility and generation. Moreover, like the God of Christian theology, this god is both immanent and transcendent.

Yet, if the mower is really Time, then the flowers that are being mowed down may be human beings. We need not wonder that the Pilgrim (and the contemporary reader of the "Dialogue") could so quickly leap to this conclusion. For the symbolism involved was (and continues to be) a commonplace. ("As for man, his days are as grass; as a flower of the field, so he flourisheth. For the wind passeth over it, and is gone; and the place therof shall know it no more" [Psalms 103:15–16]. "Man that is born of woman is of a few days, and full of trouble. He cometh forth like a flower, and is cut down" [Job 14:1–2].)

One of these flowers, then, the Pilgrim conjectures, may be his loved one: "I fear / Under some Lilly she I love / May now be growing there." (The Pilgrim is not, of course, fancying that his loved one is literally *beneath* a flower. The poet here is using the word *under* in the same sense in which he used it in "Youth and Beauty"; see above.)

He accepts the fact of death with a proper equanimity. All he now asks is that Time as reaper may take him before it takes his love. But Time cannot, of course, make any such promise, for he too is subject to the decrees of Fate. But Time can join, and does join, with the Pilgrim in voicing what, for a devoted lover, is the best state of affairs: that his death should occur before that of his beloved. (Townshend's marginal note marks those two lines as a "chorus." The modern reader would call it a "duet," but see *OED*.)

Townshend arrives at the final conceit of the poem through a kind of cinematic fade-out and dissolve. "Fate" in the line that follows (line 21) becomes transformed to the Greek Moirai, the three fatal sisters, Clotho, Lachesis, and Atropos, though it must be admitted that in this concluding line only the features of the two latter sisters even faintly emerge: those of Lachesis, who measures the thread of a mortal's life, and Atropos, the sister who cuts the thread. In this shift of figure, Time's scythe has also become Atropos's dread shears.

Do these closing lines, then, represent slovenly work? Perhaps; yet one remembers that on occasion every poet shifts abruptly from one metaphor to another—even the great John Donne himself. The point of contention will be whether the shifts in the last lines are too abrupt and so result in a confusion of the original figures rather than a shift to a new meaning. Whatever is the decision here, one must concede that Townshend lacks the tight argumentative and narrative logic of Donne's typical successes. But one could argue, on the other hand, that for Townshend's readers, Fate and the Fates, Time's scythe and Atropos's scissors, were almost interchangeable.

I have earlier suggested that Townshend's willingness to rely on his reader's acquaintance with a body of beliefs, myths, commonplaces, topics, literary conventions, and allusions sometimes tempted him to write in a sort of poetic shorthand. He must have assumed that his chosen readers would make the proper connections and manage transitions. I dare say that his seventeenth-century readers were in fact quite able to do so. If the twentieth-century reader is also to do so, he may have to do a little work. But then he has to do some work if he is to read fully Shakespeare and Milton—or, coming down to our own period, Eliot and Joyce. In their own way, they demand quite as much effort of the reader.

Whatever the merits of the three poems that we have been considering, they do have a structure, a development, that is too often lacking in the work of some of Townshend's contemporaries. A reading of George Saintsbury's *Minor Poets of the Caroline Period* makes it plain that many seventeenth-century poems are simply (or almost simply) strings of compliments or successions of conceits. A not unfair example is John Hall's "On a Gentleman and his Wife, who died both within a very few days."

> Thrice happy pair! who had and have,
> Living, one bed, now dead one grave;
> Whose love being equal, neither could
> A life unequal wish to hold,
> But left a question whether one   5
> Did follow, 'cause her mate was gone,
> Or Th'other went before to stay,
> Till that his fellow came away;
> So that one pious tear now must
> Besprinkle either parent's dust,   10

> And two great sorrows, jointly run,
> And close into a larger one,
> Or rather turn to joy, to see
> The burial but the wedding be.

One of this pair of married lovers apparently did achieve the happy state described in Townshend's poem, though we are not told which outlived the other by a few days. Yet Hall's concern is to set forth a happiness that could be enjoyed by both partners. In fact, this pair, he argues, were happy in three ways, and his poem goes on to specify how.

There are a few nice touches in the poem, for example lines 4–5, in which the poet either echoes Donne's "The Good Morrow" or perhaps independently had recourse to the same philosophical notion that Donne had used. But Hall's poem has little or no development. It simply revolves about the one noteworthy fact: that neither the husband nor the wife had had to survive the other for very long. The speaker develops three witty arguments which prove that they were finally happy in the circumstances of their deaths.

The course of the poem involves no movement toward a climactic event, and the attitude of the poet, whether or not it was his intention, is cool and detached. The poem claims to be a triumphant conclusion for the lovers but remains not much more than the celebration of an interesting oddity. The poem will seem to most readers rather cold and dry—in medieval terms, phlegmatic.

It may be useful to see how a poet nearer our own times treats a similar circumstance. I refer to one of Thomas Hardy's quiet but wonderfully resonant poems, "The Country Wedding (A Fiddler's Story)." A comparison of Hall's poem with Hardy's will point up the thinness and superficiality of Hall's.

> Little fogs were gathered in every hollow,
> But the purple hillocks enjoyed fine weather
> As we marched with our fiddles over the heather
> —How it comes back!—to their wedding that day.
>
> Our getting there brought our neighbors and all,   5
> Till, two and two, the couples stood ready.
> And her father said: "Souls, for God's sake, be steady!"
> And we strung up our fiddles, and sounded out "A."
>
> The groomsman he stared, and said, "You must follow!"
> But we'd gone to fiddle in front of the party,   10

(Our feelings as friends being true and hearty)
And fiddle in front we did — all the way.

Yes, from their door by Mill-tail-Shallow,
And up Styles-Lane, and by Front-Street houses,
Where stood maids, bachelors, and spouses,   15
Who cheered the songs that we knew how to play.

I bowed the treble before her father,
Michael the tenor in front of the lady,
The bass-viol Reub—and right well played he!—
The serpent Jim; ay, to church and back.   20

I thought the bridegroom was flurried rather,
As we kept up the tune outside the chancel,
While they were swearing things none can cancel
Inside the walls to our drumstick's whack.

"Too gay!" she pleaded. "Clouds may gather,   25
And sorrow come." But she gave in, laughing,
And by supper-time when we'd got to the quaffing
Her fears were forgot, and her smiles weren't slack.

A grand wedding 'twas! And what would follow
We never thought. Or that we should have buried her   30
On the same day with the man that married her,
A day like the first, half hazy, half clear.

Yes, little fogs were in every hollow,
Though the purple hillocks enjoyed fine weather,
When we went to play 'em to church together,   35
And carried 'em there in an after year.

    Hardy, in expanding a single anecdote, uses a great deal of circumstantial detail and a very subdued symbolism. In this poem he chooses for his observer and narrator a speaker who has not much direct involvement in the deaths he records and who makes no direct comment on the meaning of the event that has caught his interest.

    There are, of course, great differences between this poem and almost any seventeenth-century poem. The people that figure in Caroline poetry are usually people of some rank, mannered and literate, though not necessarily titled or members of the court. Hardy, on the other hand, usually writes about yeomen and the peasantry. Yet it would be easy to make too much of the differences. Hardy's world, to be sure, admits of more realism and all the quotidian details of rural life. He even makes use of West Country dialect, as when in line 7 the bride's father addresses the musicians as "Souls," meaning "Friends, fellows" (*OED* 12c, *dial.*). The language of Hardy's folk is simple and conversational, though the voice that describes and comments on their happenings is often pitched to the high style.

Yet, like the world of Herbert and Donne, Hardy's world is also a stable one, and the people who inhabit it have their immemorial folkways, customs, and appointed rituals. These are matters of great importance to a writer of Hardy's concerns and purposes. For in spite of his stress on the local peculiarities of life in rural Wessex, in writing about that life Hardy was able to comment on universal humanity. "The Country Wedding" is a case in point.

Though the fiddler who speaks the poem must have played many a bridal couple to church, the couple of whom he speaks here has a special claim on his memory, but it is only with the last two stanzas that we learn what it is. The fiddler is a garrulous countryman who insists on getting in every detail, from the day's weather to the names of the other players and the names of their instruments. He insists on maintaining the old customs: the musicians must precede the wedding party, not follow as the groomsman demands. Moreover, he is not at all shy about proclaiming the merits of his little band: they were cheered by the village folk for "the songs that [they] knew how to play" and "right well played." The fiddler has no compunction in overriding the bride's protest that the music is "Too gay" for an occasion so serious. And he was right, he tells us, for later on "she gave in, laughing." He sums up by saying "A grand wedding 'twas."

At that time he never thought—why should he have?—that he and his musicians would "in an after year" play the very same couple to church for their burial. This circumstance is what sticks in his mind and occasions his telling the story. He does not, however, tell us how the couple died—of a virulent disease that took them off together? of an accident that was fatal to both? Nor does he tell us how long they lived or whether in happiness or sorrow. The coincidence of their having been buried at the same service—it is this only that occupies his mind.

Yet, of course, his silence on these points is just as well. The poem is the stronger for leaving so much to implication and for having been focused on a single matter: the happiness in a death that leaves neither partner to grieve alone. The happiness that John Hall labored so hard to establish is here achieved, apparently without effort.

The artful poet has in this instance been wise in telling his story through the lips of an artless narrator. Yet even the fiddler's apparently irrelevant details come to have point—if not for him, at least for us. He recalls that, as it turned out, the weather on the couple's marriage day and on their funeral day was exactly alike: "little fogs were in every hollow," but the "hillocks enjoyed fine weather." An emblem of the married pair's life? Not sunshine all the way, but not cloudiness all the way either—a life not too good to be true but neither too sad to be borne?

The fiddler's little weather report, of course, proves nothing, but it may suggest much. This is particularly so when we take other matters into account, matters omitted as well as matters expressed. I have in mind the various "universalizing" details: the old-fashioned village that turns out en masse to watch the wedding procession, the ancient ritual of playing the happy couple to the church but also playing to the same church their dead bodies, the even more ancient liturgy enacted within that church, and, perhaps most of all, the fact that the husband and wife are never named. They might as well be Everyman and Everywoman.

The point of this little exercise is to demonstrate not the superiority of Hardy's methods over those of the seventeenth-century poets, but their differences. "The Country Wedding," of course, exposes all too clearly the mannered and self-conscious contrivance of Hall's poem. Moreover, if we put Hardy's poem beside Townshend's "Dialogue," it shows itself to be a much deeper and wiser commentary on human circumstances. Which is the more powerful poem is surely never in question.

But there are likenesses as well. Townshend also has found a way to focus his poem and to achieve concision. Moreover, like Hardy, he relies heavily on known associations and familiar materials, real or mythic. For Townshend, these are consciously learned, not simply absorbed from simple village life. I have here in mind not only his readers' knowledge of the Scriptures and Greek myth and legend, but the conventions and manners of seventeenth-century court life. Yet, lest we too hastily conclude that Hardy's poetry rests upon a more natural and easily apprehended base, one that is available to any reader, we might remind ourselves that a deep concern for nature and the use of immemorial rituals and fixed customs is less and less available in our restless, mobile, and urbanized twentieth-century world.

V

On a Headless (and Nameless) "Trunck"

Sir Richard Fanshawe

The Fall

The bloudy trunck of him who did possesse
    Above the rest a haplesse happy state,
    This little Stone doth Seale, but not depresse,
    And scarce can stop the rowling of his fate.
Brasse Tombes which justice hath deny'd t'his fault,   5
    The common pity to his vertues payes,
    Adorning an Imaginary vault,
    Which from our minds time strives in vaine to raze.
Ten yeares the world upon him falsly smild,
    Sheathing in fawning lookes the deadly knife   10
    Long aymed at his head; That so beguild
    It more securely might bereave his Life;
Then threw him to a Scaffold from a Throne,
Much Doctrine lyes under this little Stone.

"The Fall" is a sonnet on someone's precipitate fall from high estate. It is thus a "tragedy" of the kind told by Chaucer's Monk in *The Canterbury Tales*. But unlike the Monk, who invariably supplies the name of the tragic figure in question, Fanshawe does not tell us the name of the person who experienced this catastrophe.

In its detail, however, this sonnet is too circumstantial not to arouse the reader's curiosity about the event described. It fairly cries out for the name of the man so suddenly dragged down from a throne to the headsman's scaffold. In fact, to receive its full emotional impact as a poem we need to know who suffered the fall.

I first came upon the poem in H. J. C. Grierson's *Oxford Book of Seventeenth Century Verse,* and, as I expected, the editor supplied the needed note: "On the death of Charles I." Naturally, I assumed that the note was correct. But I quickly came to suspect that Charles I could not be the subject of the poem. So I began to examine the evidence, first the bibliographical. Obviously, if "The Fall" had been published before Charles was beheaded, he could not be the man referred to.

"The Fall" was first published in the second issue of the first edition of Fanshawe's *Il Pastor Fido,* a volume that is dated 1648. Charles, however, was not beheaded until January 30, 1649. But, of course, one has to remember that under the seventeenth-century calendar in England, the new year began not on the first of January but on March 25. Therefore, the execution of Charles occurred on January 30, 1648, old style. Assuming that the date of publication on the title page of *Il Pastor Fido* is accurate, any book dated 1648 that included a poem referring to the king's death would have to have been published before March 25. Was the issue of *Il Pastor Fido* that includes "The Fall" published before this date?

Here are the pertinent bibliographical facts. The first issue of *Il Pastor Fido* was published in 1647 by Ruth, the widow of Robert Raworth. On February 6, 1648, she assigned to Humphrey Moseley her rights in the book, along with the unsold sheets of its first printing, "together with divers other poems" of Fanshawe's, among which must have been the manuscript of "The Fall."

If we make a strict interpretation of this statement, Moseley could not have got a text of "The Fall" until February 6. Thus, the time required to set up the "divers other poems" is further shortened to a scant six weeks. Yet six weeks might have been time enough. The poet might have written "The Fall" in the week after Charles's death and included it among the "divers other poems" that Ruth Raworth assigned to Moseley, along with the unsold sheets of *Il Pastor Fido.* (All the other "divers poems" might have been written at any time earlier.) The unsold sheets of the first issue, of course, were at once ready for assembling and binding. We cannot, then, on bibliographical evidence alone, rule out the possibility that "The Fall" refers to the execution of Charles I.

When we consider the details of the poem, however, the evidence against Charles's being the victim accumulates. "The Fall" emphasizes the smallness of the stone under which the dead man's body was buried. The fact is stressed at the beginning of the poem and at the end. Such a detail ill accords with Charles's burial in the vault of Henry VIII in St. George's, Windsor.

The ninth line of the poem poses a still greater difficulty. It reads: "Ten yeares the world upon him falsely smild." Charles I reigned some twenty-four years, not ten; and if we try to save Grierson's attribution by assigning the ten years of smiling fortune to a particular period of Charles's reign—it would have to be the last ten years before his execution—the assertion dissolves into nonsense. For Charles's last decade, filled as it was with his conflicts with Parliament, the Scottish wars, the Civil War, and his imprisonment, trial, and death, is surely the least smiling period of his life.

The truth of the matter is that Fanshawe's sonnet has nothing to do with the execution of Charles I. As will soon be manifest, it comments upon the fall of Thomas Wentworth, earl of Strafford, who was impeached, tried for treason, and, on May 12, 1642, beheaded. "Ten yeares the world upon him falsly smild" makes perfect sense when applied to Strafford, who was Charles's close friend and trusted adviser during the eleven years in which the king tried to rule without a Parliament. To be more specific, Strafford's appointment as Lord Deputy of Ireland was announced on January 6, 1631. His arrest occurred in November 1641, nine years and eleven months later; his execution was ten years and some five months later—close enough to the ten years stated in the sonnet. Poets usually prefer to round off their numbers.

Fanshawe, by the way, wrote another poem on Strafford's fall. It is entitled "On the Earl of Strafford's Trial"; and a few years after Strafford's death, Fanshawe spent two years (1653–1655) in the home of Strafford's son, where he translated Camoens's *Lusiads,* which he dedicated to the younger Strafford, writing in the epistle dedicatory: "From the hour I began [this translation] to the end thereof I slept not once out of these walls." Clearly, Fanshawe was a close friend of the family and must have had Strafford's burial place, if there was merely a "little Stone," pointed out to him.

Apparently the stone placed over Strafford's grave was not only small. Perhaps it did not bear Strafford's name, for Lady Winifred Burghclere in her 1931 life of Strafford writes that she was unable to find it. She tells us that Strafford's body was borne home "so quietly for fear that the . . . brutish multitude might vent their spite on his corpse, that the place of his burying remains a mystery."[1]

Though "The Fall" is not without merit as a comment on the reversals of fortune that, with differing degrees of violence, keep occurring to this day, now that we know who the tragic figure was we are entitled to put

1. Winifred Burghclere, *Strafford,* 2:350.

ourselves more nearly into the position of Fanshawe's own chosen audience. Furthermore, the poem itself, with its amount of circumstantial detail, demands further clarification; for if we are to come nearer to a full understanding of the poem, we need to know what the various references mean.

The poem is in any case compressed and laconic. The meaning of certain lines is merely implied; the poet does not spell them out. Therefore it is thoroughly in order to see whether the standard biographies of Strafford may be able to throw further light on these details. Here we are fortunate. Lady Burghclere's two-volume biography, already referred to, offers a very full account of Strafford's life and fall from power. Dame Veronica Wedgwood's *Strafford* (1935; revised 1961 as *Thomas Wentworth*) is the work of an esteemed historian who is a recognized authority on this period. She can be counted on for an estimate about as free from either Royalist or Puritan bias as one can hope to find.

According to both these biographers, Strafford was a man of great parts, attractive, a persuasive orator, and perhaps Charles's wisest political adviser. His "thorough" policy in Ireland was not oppressive of the Irish folk. Strafford gave them a good administration and a measure of protection from the great landowners. Dame Veronica Wedgwood writes:

> Though Strafford's policy had been, inevitably, based on the fundamental wrong inherent in the seizure of Irish land, [Strafford] had believed and had tried to establish a standard of justice other than the right of the strongest, and he had worked hard to create an economy and a society in which life would be better for the native Irish as well as for the English settlers. Nor for many years would Ireland again enjoy so great a measure of prosperity and order as it had done under his administration.[2]

Strafford was a strong-minded man. He made many enemies, including John Pym, that powerful figure in the Parliamentary party. His enemies were relentless in their efforts not only to get Strafford out of power but to take his life. It is not too extreme a statement to say that his trial for treason amounted to a case of judicial murder, a kind of lynching. Yet for a number of years before his fall, he was able to frustrate all efforts to destroy him. His talents as an orator and his brilliance as a leader impressed everyone, and were admitted and feared by his opponents. But that very recognition of his powers did much to ensure his death, for his enemies did not feel truly safe as long as he was alive.

2. Cecily Veronica Wedgwood, *Thomas Wentworth, First Earl of Strafford, a Revaluation*, 392–93.

In view of Fanshawe's close friendship with Strafford and his family, the sonnet on his death shows great restraint. There is no obvious outpouring of grief or violent resentment. The poem belongs in the tradition of the laconic epitaph, condensed, terse, with its conclusion in a couplet that has an epigrammatic bite. It has the quality of reserve that we associate with an observer who speaks with considerable detachment. This quality would be sufficiently evident even if we knew nothing of the poet's personal relationship to the man who died.

Having learned about the closeness of the friendship between Fanshawe and Strafford, our estimate of the poem may or may not be increased, but we have certainly learned something about the poet. He could control, in the interest of his poem, the emotions of grief and outrage that quite obviously he must have felt. A more cynical reader, of course, might interpret matters somewhat differently: he might opine that Fanshawe controlled his emotion of outrage out of sheer prudence.

It may be worth noting that—whatever the motive, whether for aesthetic or prudential reasons—Fanshawe's poem on Strafford's trial shows the same restraint and reserve. There is not a sentence in that poem that denounces the unfairness of the prosecution of Strafford or the flimsiness of the charges brought against him. Instead, the poem is wholly devoted to a commendation of Strafford's statesmanship and his gallantry as he faced his enemies in the trial. The poet proclaims him "a *Souldier* and an *Oratour*." He is praised because he did not cut and run, as he might have done, and thus have avoided the trial that was to condemn him. Instead, he stood his trial, and when condemned to die, he turned "his conquering *Eloquence*" against himself in beseeching the king whom he had served so loyally to give assent to his death. The 1648 text prints a note beside these lines which reads as follows: "The Earles pathetical Letter to the King, which is to be seene in print wherein hee begges of his Majesty, to pass the bill for his death, to quiet the Kingdomes."

The whole emphasis of the poem is thus on the gallantry of the man when in the hands of his enemies, and the nobility with which he accepted his death. Marvell, a year or two later, was to emphasize Charles's behavior in the hands of his enemies, and the noble dignity with which he laid down his head on the executioner's block. Marvell also echoes in his poem the metaphor that Fanshawe elaborates in "On the Earle of Straffords Tryall": Strafford "affects a labour'd Scene." Yet if it will not prove to be a comedy with its happy ending, he will endeavor "To make it of all *Tragedies* the best." And finally,

> . . . for his lifes *last act,*
> *Times* shall admiring read it, and *this age*
> Though now it *hisse, claps* when he leaves the Stage.

Did Marvell consciously borrow Fanshawe's figure when he wrote his "Horatian Ode"? One cannot say with certainty that he did. In an era in which the theater had been so powerful an influence and so popular, such a simile was obviously available to everyone. It seems likely, however, that Marvell borrowed the stanza form of his "Horatian Ode" from Fanshawe. In 1946 I pointed out that Fanshawe had used it in several of his translations of Horace (published in 1652); and Fanshawe's modern editor, N. W. Bawcutt, writes that "Fanshawe . . . anticipated more than once the stanza form used by Marvell in his 'Horatian Ode.'" But he adds that "it seems unlikely that Marvell borrowed it from him." Why unlikely? The form was rarely used in this period, and Marvell, during his early years, seems to have known well all the Royalist poets. Moreover, as William Simeone has pointed out, Fanshawe employed the form very early. It is used in his "Oade," which Simeone believes was written as early as 1625.[3]

At this point it is time to turn from speculations about Fanshawe, the author of the poem, to the poem itself, including its nuances. Here a knowledge of Strafford's life and of the history of the period may throw light on some details of the poem; and, one should point out, the details of the poem may just possibly also throw light upon biography and history.

An example of this latter circumstance may be provided in the first five words of the sonnet, "The bloudy trunck of him." These words alert the reader immediately to the fact that the unnamed man died by beheading and thus provide a startling and almost shocking opening for the poem. But they may also just possibly preserve a historical fact not mentioned by Strafford's biographers: namely, that the severed head might not have been returned with the body to Strafford's family. Strafford had been convicted of high treason, and at this time the heads of those guilty of treason were exhibited over Traitors' Gate at the Southwark end of London Bridge. But perhaps Strafford was spared this indignity.

In line 2, "haplesse happy" is the kind of word play that the poets of the period delighted in. Both words derive from the same root, the Old Norse *hap,* which meant simply chance or luck, good or bad. He was

---

3. N. W. Bawcutt, ed., *Sir Richard Fanshawe: Shorter Poems and Translations,* xii; William Simeone, "A Probably Antecedent of Marvell's Horatian Ode."

hapless (unlucky) to have been so happy (lucky). The play on words heightens the point that the poet is making: the very good fortune that Strafford enjoyed made him a special target for his enemies. The paradox looks forward to lines 9–10, the falsely smiling countenance of the world and its "fawning lookes" that "beguild" him into underestimating the real danger in which he stood or—what amounts to the same thing— to overestimating his own power to cope with his enemies. (This latter point is, though with a different tonal modulation, the thesis of the poem that Fanshawe wrote on Strafford's trial.)

With line 3, we come to the first mention of the little stone beneath which he was buried. The stone seals him off from the world that destroyed him, but does not "depresse" his dead body. The hope that the earth will lie lightly on a loved one's body has a long tradition behind it. Instances could be provided ranging from Herrick's "Upon a Child that Died" (which concludes with "Give her strewings, but not stir / The earth that lightly covers her") at one extreme, to, at the other, the mock epitaph on Van Brugh, the architect of Blenheim Palace, with its closing petition, "Lie heavy on him, earth, for he / Laid many a heavy load on thee." Yet "but not depresse" his fate has a more important significance: the little stone, for all its humiliating meagerness, cannot degrade the true merit of such a man as Strafford was.

The poet, however, has not yet done with the unimpressive gravestone. The stone seems entirely too small to have stopped "the rowling of [Strafford's] fate." The reference, of course, is to the wheel of fortune, the revolution of which may lift a man to the heights or throw him to the depths. Is the underlying idea that the little stone, a mere pebble on the road of history, has, nevertheless, been able to arrest fortune's wheel so powerfully and suddenly that Strafford, high on that wheel, has been hurled "to a Scaffold" from his place beside the throne?

If this is the tenor of the metaphor, the poet has developed it into a very bold one, a metaphysical conceit no less. The reader may have his doubts as to its success, but in any case this complicated figure calls in question any judgment that Fanshawe was "unaffected by Metaphysical poetry."

Another rather elaborate figure is developed in the second quatrain: though justice has denied to Strafford a tomb worthy of his rank and merit, "common pity" pays to the dead Strafford "Brasse Tombes." If *pays* seems to be used here in a very strained sense, one should point out that the *OED* provides clarification. Sense 2 of *pay* means "gives (to a person) what is due . . . as return for services done."

These "Brasse Tombes," to be sure, exist only in our minds and so adorn an imaginary vault, one in which no actual body reposes. Nevertheless, just because they are ideal, such funerary monuments will endure longer than real brass. Young John Milton had scorned material stone for building a monument to Shakespeare's "honoured bones"; that poet's enduring monument has been erected in the "wonder and astonishment" of the readers of his works.

Fanshawe was also well aware that many centuries earlier Horace had claimed to have erected a monument more enduring than brass. In fact, Fanshawe translated the Latin poet's *"Exegi monumentum aere perennius"* thus:

> A Work out-lasting Brass, and higher
> Than Regal Pyramid's proud Spire,
> I have absolved. Which storming Winds
> The Sea that Turrets undermines,
> Tract of innumerable daies,
> Nor the rout of Times can raze.

The last line of this translation, the reader will note, echoes the eighth line of "The Fall": "time strives in vaine to raze."

Eventually a monument to Strafford was erected in the Wentworth chapel of the ruined church at Wentworth Woodhouse. But, as Dame Veronica Wedgwood put it in 1935, the "rich monument covers an empty vault, for the resting place of Wentworth's body is hidden now from the curiosity of the world as it was three hundred years ago from the insulting malice of his enemies."[4] That monument was set up many years after Strafford's death and Fanshawe's death. Sir Nikolaus Pevsner in his *Yorkshire: The West Riding* dates the statue of Strafford and his lady some time after 1685, some forty years after his death.

On the basis of further investigation which disclosed further evidence, Wedgwood wrote in 1961:

> The body of the great Earl of Strafford was left where it had been quietly interred after his death. Legends grew up, that he had been buried secretly to preserve his resting-place from the desecrating hands of enemies. Some said that Elizabeth, his widow, who outlived him forty-seven years, was buried in the same secret grave with him near her dower house in the Church of Hooton Roberts. But the story

4. Cecily Veronica Wedgwood, *Strafford, 1593–1641,* 344–45.

is baseless. There was no mystery about his burial place until later generations began to fabricate it. He lies in the family vault of the little church at Wentworth Woodhouse.[5]

This statement would seem to be decisive, but in Dame Helen Gardner's collection *The Metaphysical Poets,* first published in 1957, reprinted in 1959, 1961, and 1964, and revised in 1966, Dame Helen states in a footnote, "It is not known where he [the earl of Strafford] was buried; the tomb erected at Wentworth Woodhouse after the restoration is a cenotaph."[6] She seems to repeat the old story, for the note offers no new evidence and makes no reference to Dame Veronica Wedgwood's statement in her revised work, *Thomas Wentwood.*

I have thus far sought in vain for information that would confirm or contradict Dame Veronica's final conclusion. Ms. Maija Jansson of the Yale Department of History has kindly called my attention to two items that may have some bearing on the problem. The first is a statement made in the Diary of John Moore. In the Harleian MS. 478, f. 66b-67A, he says that on the scaffold Strafford "desyred the sheriffe that after execution his bodie might be peacably conveyed away." But nothing is further said as to whether the sheriff's order was carried out.

The second item is a passage printed in *A Complete Collection of State Trials and Proceedings for High Treason,* compiled by T. B. Howell: "His [Wentworth's] body was afterwards embalmed, and appointed to be carried into Yorkshire, there to be buried amongst his ancestors."[7] Again the statement concerns what was appointed to be done and nothing about its accomplishment. But the fact that nothing is said about anything having gone amiss strengthens the presumption that the earl's wishes were indeed carried out.

When a modern reader of "The Fall" reflects upon line 5 he may well be puzzled at Fanshawe's use of the word *justice.* Granted the poet's tone of studied detachment, how could he write that it was justice that denied Strafford a tomb worthy of his virtues? Did the poet trust that his reader would realize that *justice* was here spoken with bitter irony?

Perhaps Fanshawe did assume that his reader would interpret the word in this fashion. But the modern reader may need to be told that in Fanshawe's time *justice* could signify no more than "the administration

5. Wedgwood, *Thomas Wentworth,* 395.
6. Helen Gardner, ed., *The Metaphysical Poets,* rev. ed., 174.
7. T. B. Howell, comp., *A Complete Collection of State Trials and Proceedings for High Treason,* sec. 1525.

of law, or the forms and processes attending it; judicial proceedings" (*OED* 5). Perhaps the poet chose *justice* deliberately because it allowed the reader to take the meaning to be no more than "judicial process," but in this context it shimmers with ironical overtones of true justice denied.

To some of Fanshawe's readers the word *justice* would arouse bitter memories indeed. While Strafford's attainder was debated in the House of Lords, the London mob "stormed Westminster, crying 'Justice, justice.'" When fifty-nine of the Peers had the hardihood to vote against the Bill of Attainder, their names were posted as "Enemies of justice." As his end drew near, Strafford's only hope was the king's refusal to give assent to the bill. Hoping to pacify the kingdoms, Strafford wrote to the king (see above) asking that he sign the bill (and so, in effect, Strafford's own death warrant). Charles was at length persuaded. The document he signed begins with the words: "I did yesterday satisfie the Justice of the Kingdome by passing of the Bill of Attaindour against the Earle of Strafford." The king coupled with it an appeal for mercy. He hoped that Strafford's peers would be satisfied with the royal promise that never again would Strafford hold office. The king's letter concludes: "but if no lesse than his Lyfe can satisfie my People, I must say 'Fiat Justitia.'"

So much for the personal and historical associations that the poem presumably evokes in Fanshawe's readers who were familiar with the events to which the poem refers. But in taking account of these, we must not pass too lightly over the skill the poet has shown in marshaling and deploying the rhetorical energies of the poem. Thus, the sonnet is thoroughly unified: it ends with the same circumstance with which it began, the size of the stone under which Strafford was buried. The sonnet also manages expertly the matter of emphasis. The poem opens by flinging at the reader's feet the bloody trunk of a man and ends by telling us from where it was thrown.

As for the identity of the headless trunk, one may summarize by saying it is certainly not that of Charles I, and the case for its being that of the earl of Strafford seems very likely. But I must now tell the reader that "The Fall" is actually a translation of a sonnet by Luis de Góngora, one that commemorates the death of his friend Rodrigo Calderón, who was for a long time a favorite at the Spanish court but eventually fell from power and was beheaded in 1621, some twenty years before Strafford's execution.

En La Muerte De D. Rodrigo Calderón

Sella el tronco sangriento, no le oprime,
De aquel dichosamente desdichado,
Que de las inconstancias de su hado
Esta piçarra apenas le redime;
Piedad comun en vez de la sublime
Urna que el escarmiento le ha negado,
Padron le erige en bronce imaginado,
Que en vano el tiempo las memorias lime.
Risueño con el, tanto como falso,
El tiempo, quatro lustros en la risa,
El cuchillo quiçà embainaua agudo.
Del sìtiàl despues al cadahalso
Precipitado, ô quanto nos auisa!
ô quanta trompa es su exemplo mudo!

Fanshawe served as secretary to the English ambassador to Spain in 1635–1638, and in the last year was chargé d'affaires. After the Restoration he was ambassador to Portugal and, later, to Spain. As one would expect, he had a sound grasp of the Spanish language and of the happenings at the Spanish court. He translated a number of Góngora's poems.

What happens, then, to the elaborate case we have built up for Strafford as the victim in "The Fall"? Where does it leave us? Well, actually, it leaves matters very close to where they were. Fanshawe's translation is not slavishly close, and he makes some significant alterations in Góngora's poem. Thus, the emphasis on the meager stone is almost entirely Fanshawe's contribution. He has radically changed the final line. Most significantly, he has altered Góngora's "quatro lustros" (that is to say, twenty years), to ten years, in which the world "falsly smild" on the favorite.

In 1964 Fanshawe's editor, N. W. Bawcutt, provided the following note: "Title in *E* [Bodleian MS. Firth c.1.:] *A great Fauorit beheaded.* From Góngora, *En la muerte de don Rodrigo Calderon,* 'Sella al tronco sangriento, no le oprime'. . . . Fanshawe may have been struck by its applicability to the Earl of Strafford." Surely, the last sentence is too cautious. Clearly Fanshawe has remodeled the poem on Calderón to make it apply closely and accurately to Strafford.

Fanshawe's most striking alteration of Góngora's sonnet was his alteration of the twenty years in which fortune smiled on Calderón to the ten years of power accorded to Strafford. Another of the alterations Fanshawe made is interesting. Góngora has little to say about the smallness of the stone that sealed Calderón's grave. (It is possible that the observation made in the first line of his sonnet—the seal does not "oppress" the body it covers—may hint at its small size.) But in "The Fall" Fanshawe insists on its small size. In line 3 he writes "*This little Stone,*" and he returns to the matter in the concluding line of the poem: "*Much Doctrine Lyes under this little Stone.*"

One is tempted to speculate. Was Strafford's body with an obscure marker temporarily buried in a secret place known only to his family and close friends? If so, Fanshawe as a family friend would have known the location of the temporary grave and his sonnet entitled "The Fall" might thus preserve a detail that has hitherto escaped the notice of the historians.

Yet such is pure speculation, and it is more profitable to turn back to fact and to look at a poem written by Fanshawe that undoubtedly has to do with Strafford and the events leading up to his execution.

On the Earle of Straffords Tryall

The Earle yet made a gallant stand, to be
Judg'd by *one* Kingdome, and *arraign'd* by *three.*
He might have fled at first, or made his skreene
A Royall Master, or a Gracious Queene;
But this had been the *Touch-stone* to decline,
T'ingage in Mortalls Quarrels, Powers Divine.
As artlesse Poets *Jove* or *Juno* use,
To play the Mid-wife to their labouring Muse.
No, he affects a labour'd Scene, and not
To *cut,* but to *untye* the Gordian knot.
Then if 'twill prove no *Comedy,* at least
To make it of all *Tragedies* the best.
And that hee'l doe; I know not what past fact
May speake him lesse, but for his lifes *last act,*
Times shall admiring read it, and *this age*
Though now it *hisse, claps* when he leaves the Stage;
So *stand* or *fall,* none *stood* so, or so *fell*;
This farre-fam'd *Tryall* hath no paralell.
  But if i' th' *Senate,* Cæsar had been *try'd,*
As he was *stab'd,* whilst with their hands fast ty'd,
The Armies had lookt on, and left the *Cause*
Of *Rome* to *Tully* onely, and the *Lawes,*

> Thus had great *Julius* spoke, and lookt; distill'd
> *Pharsalia, Munda, Thapsus* hard-fought Feld,
> All into Speeches; and free *Cato* mov'd,
> (Though he could never feare) yet then t' have *lov'd,*
> And *pittyed* him: For mixt of *Peace* and *Warre,*
> He was a *Souldier* and an *Oratour.*
> A *Cæsar?* or a *Strafford? Hee* resolv'd,
> T' abide no *tryall: This,* to be *absolv'd*
> Or *dye.* Herein more like to *Otho* farre,
> Who gave his blood to quench a *Civill Warre.*
> Nor shall he dye, unlesse these broyles t'asswage
> A yet *more Civill Warre* himselfe shall wage,
> Turne (what hee us'd so well for his defence)
> Against *himselfe,* his conquering *Eloquence,*
> Spend his whole stock of favour too, to bring
> To the *Three Kingdoms* a *fourth* Power, *the King:*
> A *Fourth Estate* adde to the *Parliament:*
> And to the *Royall* give his *owne assent.*
> So fell great *Rome* her selfe, opprest at length
> By the united *Worlds,* and her *owne* strength.

This poem is not so graceful nor so elegantly compact as is "The Fall." It is more closely tied to the sequence of historical events. It occupies itself with references to events and to characters in Roman history: to Caesar, Cicero, Cato, and the Roman emperor M. Salvius Otho, who voluntarily gave up his own life to prevent the continuance of a civil war and further losses to his faithful followers.

As a poem, "On the Earle of Strafford's Tryall" is not one of Fanshawe's best, but it makes quite clear that Fanshawe was in full command of the facts that led to Strafford's fall; it stresses those features of Strafford's conduct that Fanshawe found truly praiseworthy, and it makes clear that the apparent reserve that characterizes "The Fall" does not indicate any lack of sympathy on Fanshawe's part for the plight of his friend.

Postscript (1991)

Just as the page proof for this volume appeared on my desk, I heard from Mr. Kim Collis, the archivist of the Wentworth papers. He writes that he found among the papers only three items that may have a bearing on the earl's place of burial. The first is a letter of 1923 that indicates that Wentworth's grave "in the old church at Wentworth" was excavated some years earlier to check whether or not it contained a body. But the letter does not mention whether or not a body was found. The second item concerns a description of the "opening of my Lord's body" dated May 13, 1642. (Wentworth had been executed just a year before, on May 12, 1641.) The third item is a list of monumental inscriptions inside the old church at Wentworth. The only one that might possibly refer to the earl reads as follows: "This is the monument of Thomas Wentworth of Wentworth Esquire whose soul is in the [indecipherable] of God and his body which was made of [indecipherable]."

These bits of evidence are scarcely decisive, though they do suggest that the earl's final resting place is at or at least near the old church at Wentworth. But the first two items would suggest that there had indeed been doubts as to where the body had been deposited. Indeed, they may offer some room for thinking that the body might for a time have been kept in a secret place—something that Fanshawe's poem would itself suggest.

Dame Veronica Wedgwood kindly had someone answer my letter of inquiry directed to her. She wrote that she was not now able to recover the process through which she had come to her conclusion in her book published in 1961. But she believes that this was the proper conclusion. Perhaps it was, and perhaps it is wise to leave the matter where she left it.

VI

A Philosophical Poet

Lord Herbert of Cherbury

The poetry written by Edward, Lord Herbert of Cherbury, differs radically from the far more celebrated poetry of his brother George. The lives of the two brothers differed to as great a degree. Lord Herbert was a soldier, a courtier, and a man prompt to react to any affront to his honor. He was quick to challenge his opponent to a duel, and there were a number of such episodes in his early life.

Lord Herbert was also a traveler, quite at home on the Continent and a close friend of several French noblemen. He served twice as the English ambassador at Paris. Herbert's well-known and highly interesting autobiography (which was first published by Horace Walpole in 1764) constitutes a rather elegant feat of not ungraceful braggadocio. Herbert was fully aware of his own merits.

His saintly brother George had also begun his life with bright hopes for preferment at court. Yet after his decision to enter the Church, he became a dedicated Anglican priest and was content to serve out his days as vicar of the obscure parish of Bemerton. Whereas George's poetry is almost a model of direct, unstrained, uncluttered verse, that of Edward is often contorted and convoluted. It fairly flaunts the author's learning. Such at least is the consensus of present-day opinions. It is startling, therefore, to note that Lord Herbert's editor, G. C. Moore Smith, as late as 1923 wrote: "For my part, while admitting the unequal character of Herbert's verses, I am inclined to claim that in poetic feeling and art Edward Herbert soars above his brother George."

I have remarked that Lord Herbert's poetry is ambitious—consciously so. It is also, much of it at least, derivative of the poetry of Ben Jonson and John Donne. As an example of Jonson's influence, consider the following lyric, which Moore Smith has entitled "Ditty."

> Deep Sighs, Records of my unpitied Grief,
> Memorials of my true, though hopeless Love,

> Keep time with my sad thoughts, till wish'd Relief
> My long despairs for vain and causless prove.
>
> Yet if such hap never to you befall,
> I give you leave, break time, break heart and all.

Let us put beside it one of the songs in Jonson's *Cynthia's Revels*:

> Slow, slow, fresh fount, keepe time with my salt teares;
> Yet slower, yet, o faintly gentle springs:
> List to the heauy part the musique beares,
>   "Woe weepes out her diuision, when shee sings.
>   Droupe hearbs, and flowres;
>   Fall griefe in showres;
>   "Our beauties are not ours:
>   O, I could still
> (Like melting snow upon some craggie hill,)
>   drop, drop, drop, drop,
> Since natures pride is, now, a wither'd daffodill.

Though its derivation is obvious, Herbert's lyric is not unworthy of its
model.

Herbert's "A Sinner's Lament" even more clearly reveals the influence
of one of Donne's sonnets:

> If poysonous mineralls, and if that tree
> Whose fruit threw death on else immortall us,
> If lecherous goats, if serpents envious
> Cannot be damn'd, Alas, why should I bee?
> Why should intent or reason, borne in mee,
> Make sinnes, else equall, in mee, more Heinous?
> And mercy being easie, and glorious
>
> To God, in his sterne wrath, why threatens hee?
> But who am I, that dare dispute with thee?
> O God, Oh! of thine onely worthy blood,
> And my teares, make a heavenly Lethean flood,
> And drowne in it my sinnes blacke memorie.
> That thou remember them, some claime as debt,
> I think it mercy if thou will forget.

Here is Herbert's poem:

A Sinner's Lament

Lord, thus I sin, repent, and sin again,
  As if Repentance only were, in me,
Leave for new Sin; thus do I entertain
  My short time, and thy Grace, abusing thee,
  And thy long-suffering; which though it be
Ne'r overcome by Sin, yet were in vain,
  If tempted oft: thus we our Errours see

Before our Punishment, and so remain
  Without Excuse; and, Lord, in them 'tis true,
Thy Laws are just, but why dost thou distrain
  Ought else for life, save life? That is thy due:
The rest thou mak'st us owe, and mayst to us
As well forgive; But oh! my sins renew,
Whil'st I do talk with my Creator thus.

Nevertheless, Herbert did develop a characteristic style of his own, and his best poems (though they bristle with difficulties) are worth exploring. Herbert's involved syntax is a recurrent problem to any reader. For example, though "To his Watch, when he could not sleep" opens brilliantly and closes with some resonant lines, after a strenuous wrestle with the meaning of the poem this reader has had to admit defeat.

Another obstacle is Herbert's habit of making recondite references to Platonic and neo-Platonic philosophy. But the barrier that most often bars access to Herbert's meaning is of a different sort: the words that cause the trouble, though still current, make sense only in their obsolete seventeenth-century meanings.

It would be foolish, of course, to blame Herbert for not having fore-seen the radical changes in the meaning of his vocabulary. After all, a poet writes out of his own era. Nevertheless, if one really hopes to make sense of Herbert's poems, he must expect to keep the *OED* at his elbow. Obscure sentences and sometimes whole stanzas become miraculously transparent once one has recovered the precise meaning of a single word. This problem is not, of course, peculiar to Herbert. One remembers how much glossing Shakespeare's works require. Yet in my experience the problem is much greater with Lord Herbert than it is with Donne or Ben Jonson or Herbert's brother George.

Herbert's "A Meditation of His Wax-candle Burning Out" provides a signal instance of the difficulties that encumber Herbert's poetry. It is a quite original poem and, once unfolded, turns out to be thoroughly intelligible. The burning candle flame provides a sound example of man's life on earth. The "earthly parts" of the candle will finally lie in ashes, once the burning has been completed. But the candle's flame, like man's soul, aspires toward a higher realm: the fire seeks to rise above the candle and the smoke ascends still higher. But Herbert will not be content with any of the simpler developments of this analogy. All sorts of further details beckon to him. For example, like the candle, the human being is made up of the four elements, earth, water, air, and fire; and not only is the soul immortal but the four elements have their immortality too. The elements are able not only to maintain their original character but to generate other things. The heat and light that they generate can produce meteors and indeed occasionally a meteor brighter than a star. Such, for instance, was the brilliant star that burned in the constellation of Cassiopeia for some months in 1572. (Today we have been taught to call such a phenomenon a supernova.)

The body of the human being is of course inevitably to fall into dissolution. Herbert knows the doctrine that the unnatural union of "unequal parts thus commix'd" cannot be permanent. Moreover, he regards the elements as not merely docile and passive but active and capable of discordancy. Yet if the various elements that make up our bodies are after our death free to revert each to its proper place, "What may we not hope from our part divine?" Bits of the natural science of the day, borrowings from Plato, items from the New Testament, and so on are interwoven in this carefully argued poem.

My original intention was to show the development accorded by Herbert by making a full explication of the poem with copious references to the *OED* for the meanings that Herbert assigned to many of his terms. But I have concluded that it is better not to ask so much of my readers here. Herbert's masterpiece "An Ode upon a Question Moved, Whether Love should continue forever" will provide a sufficiently adequate example of Herbert's demands upon the reader. But with this poem one can make a much better claim for its success as poetry and not simply a rather hollow triumph of philosophy over poetry.

The title of the poem is thoroughly characteristic of its author. Yet it might have come right out of a medieval university hall against the counterarguments of a fellow student. Nevertheless, the situation described in the opening stanzas is traditional in poetry and even conven-

tional: a young man and young woman, very much in love with each
other, are out for a walk in the springtime countryside.

> Having interr'd her Infant-birth,
>   The watry ground that late did mourn,
>   Was strew'd with flow'rs for the return
> Of the wish'd Bridegroom of the earth.
>
> The well accorded Birds did sing   5
>   Their hymns unto the pleasant time,
>   And in a sweet consorted chime
> Did welcom in the chearful Spring.
>
> To which, soft whistles of the Wind,
>   And warbling murmurs of a Brook,   10
>   And vari'd notes of leaves that shook,
> An harmony of parts did bind.
>
> While doubling joy unto each other,
>   All in so rare concent was shown,
>   No happiness that came alone,   15
> Nor pleasure that was not another.
>
> When with a love none can express
>   That mutually happy pair,
>   Melander and Celinda fair,
> The season with their loves did bless.   20
>
> Walking thus towards a pleasant Grove,
>   Which did, it seem'd, in new delight
>   The pleasures of the time unite,
> To give a triumph to their love, . . .

As has often been noted, Herbert's "Ode" in many respects resembles
Donne's "Ecstasy," and almost certainly was influenced by it. Both
H. J. C. Grierson and Dame Helen Gardner point out parallels between
the two poems, including neo-Platonic elements shared by them. In
both poems there is a dialogue between the lovers, spoken or unspoken,
and both poems vindicate the purity of a love expressed by and through
the senses. But as examination will make plain, there are marked differences not only in the modes of expression but also in the poets'
treatments of the general theme. Thus, in "The Ecstasy" the problem of
what happens after death to human love is not dealt with, whereas in
"An Ode" this matter is the lovers' main preoccupation. (In "The Ec-

stasy" the speaker seems to take it simply for granted that the love that bound the lovers together will endure beyond the grave.)

The opening stanzas of "An Ode" hold few problems for the modern reader; yet some words may need to be glossed. The "Infant-birth" which had been "interr'd" by the "watry ground" presumably refers to the seeds of last year's flowers, which, having been buried during the winter season, now cover their burial places with fresh blossoms. The phrase "well accorded Birds" (line 5) refers to birds singing in tune (*OED* 3); and "consorted" (line 7) is an early variant of the modern word *concert* and means a "harmonious chime" (also *OED* 3). The "notes" (line 11) are, of course, notes of music. "Concent" (line 14) means "concord" or "harmony" (*OED* 2).

The happy lovers, entwined in each others' arms, listen to the sounds of springtime with which they themselves are utterly in tune. They bless the season with their love (line 20). A bold (though perhaps unwarranted) reading would assume that the lovers have acquired through the power of their love a quasi-divinity which confers upon them the power to bestow blessings. Until much later than Herbert's time *bless* was usually associated with the action of a deity. Herbert's lovers would seem to be in the emotional state described by a poet of our own time, W. B. Yeats:

> My body of a sudden blazed;
> And twenty minutes more or less
> It seemed so great my happiness
> That I was blessed and could bless.

Even a poet of our own time was familiar with the doctrine and believed he had experienced the sense of being able to confer a blessing. But Yeats was, of course, a very special case, particularly in his strong ties with ancient traditions.

In Herbert's poem the lovers at length stop and repose on the grass.

> They stay'd at last, and on the Grass   25
>   Reposed so, as o'r his breast
>   She bow'd her gracious head to rest,
> Such a weight as no burden was.
>
> While over eithers compass'd waste
>   Their folded arms were so compos'd,   30
>   As if in straitest bonds inclos'd,
> They suffer'd for joys they did taste.

> Long their fixt eyes to Heaven bent,
>   Unchanged, they did never move,
>   As if so great and pure a love   35
> No glass but it could represent. . . .

"Gracious" (line 27) might be held to strengthen the notion that (in Melander's mind at least) Celinda has taken on the character of a goddess. But the meaning may simply be "graceful" (*OED* 2b).

Line 32 ("They suffer'd for joys they did taste") raises some difficulties. Does it mean: The joys they now tasted were so intense as to be actually painful? ("Pleasing pain" is a paradox of long lineage in poetry.) Or does the line mean: Their yearning fully to experience joys of which they now had only a foretaste was so intense as to be painful? Under *taste* the *OED* (7) cites the meaning "to take only as much as is sufficient to perceive the taste of."

Either reading accords with the general development of the argument of the poem, for, as we shall see, the basic point of concern in the poem is whether the joys that the lovers now experience in life will survive the grave. The alternative view would be that in the afterlife those joys would be superseded by a purely spiritual union. This latter possibility is Celinda's concern and motivates her anxious question to her lover. In a passage again reminiscent of Donne's "Ecstasy" the lovers look up toward heaven as if it were the only "glass" (mirror) that could "represent" so pure a love. "Represent," I suppose, is to be pronounced as today in the sense of "re-present," meaning to give back, to reflect what was presented to it by one's looking into it. The reference is most apposite, for the issue is whether the love which seems to the lovers a heavenly joy will in fact find a place in heaven.

> When with a sweet, though troubled look,
>   She first brake silence, saying, Dear friend,
>   O that our love might take no end,
> Or never had beginning took!   40
>
> I speak not this with a false heart,
>   (Wherewith his hand she gently strain'd)
>   Or that would change a love maintain'd
> With so much faith on either part.
>
> Nay, I protest, though Death with his   45
>   Worst Counsel should divide us here,
>   His terrors could not make me fear,
> To come where your lov'd presence is.

> Only if loves fire with the breath
>   Of life be kindled, I doubt,   50
>   With our last air 'twill be breath'd out,
> And quenched with the cold of death.
>
> That if affection be a line,
>   Which is clos'd up in our last hour;
>   Oh how 'twould grieve me, any pow'r   55
> Could force so dear a love as mine! . . .

Celinda is genuinely troubled. Better their love had never begun at all if it is only mortal and will perish with the corrupting body. In line 45 "protest," of course, has the meaning "solemnly avow." "Counsel," in line 46, must here have the now obsolete meaning of "a private, or secret purpose, design" (*OED* 5). In line 50 "doubt" has its older meaning, "fear." Celinda's argument is a shrewd one: if the fire of love only begins with the breath of life, why will it not cease with the exhalation of our last breath? Herbert, and his readers, all sound Latinists, knew that the word *expire,* already by this time carrying the meaning "to die," meant literally in Latin "to breathe out," to "exhale."

Celinda's account of the creation of love in the human heart is reminiscent of the account of the creation of Adam in Genesis. If love is breathed into the heart not by God in this instance but by life, what reason is there to hope that love will not expire when life breathes out its last gasp?

Herbert's locution (lines 53–54) in which a line is conceived as "clos'd up" may seem odd to the twentieth-century reader. But in Herbert's time "to close up" could mean simply to "end or complete (something)" (*OED* 21d). In line 56 "force" means to "constrain, by force" (*OED* 3); in line 59 "intent" carries its earlier meaning of "bent (upon), resolved" (*OED* 1).

> She scarce had done, when his shut eyes
>   An inward joy did represent,
>   To hear *Celinda* thus intent
> To a love he so much did prize.   60
>
> Then with a look, it seem'd, deny'd
>   All earthly pow'r but hers, yet so,
>   As if to her breath he did ow
> This borrowd life, he thus repli'd; . . .

Melander is overcome with joy at the depth of Celinda's love as expressed in her anguished question. His answering look proclaims that he is now bereft of any life of his own. Such life as he now possesses he owes to the breath with which Celinda has uttered the undying character of her love for him. Thus, his long reply to her is to be regarded as an inspired utterance. Celinda has, in effect, become his muse. His words are not merely his own but derived from her.

In making this interpretation of lines 61–64, I should explain that I interpret "yet" in line 62 as lacking the adversative force which it usually has in present-day English. I take it to mean here "furthermore, moreover" (*OED* 1). This is, by the way, its earliest meaning.

Such an account of the effect of Celinda's speech on her lover (that is, breathing a new life into him) echoes, of course, lines 49–50, where the breath of life kindles the fire of love. The repetition of the image as used here involves one of those reversals in which the metaphysical poets delighted: the image of bestowing the breath of life in the first instance to voice the possibility of the death of love becomes, in the second, Melander's assertion that love will never die.

> O you, wherein, they say, Souls rest,   65
>   Till they descend pure heavenly fires,
>   Shall lustful and corrupt desires
> With your immortal seed be blest?
>
> And shall our Love, so far beyond
>   That low and dying appetite,   70
>   And which so chast desires unite,
> Not hold in an eternal bond?
>
> Is it, because we should decline,
>   And wholly from our thoughts exclude
>   Objects that may the sense delude,   75
> And study only the Divine?
>
> No sure, for if none can ascend
>   Ev'n to the visible degree
>   Of things created, how should we
> The invisible comprehend?   80
>
> Or rather since that Pow'r exprest
>   His greatness in his works alone,
>   B'ing here best in his Creatures known,
> Why is he not lov'd in them best?
>
> But is't not true, which you pretend,   85
>   That since our love and knowledge here,

Only as parts of life appear,
So they with it should take their end.

O no, Belov'd, I am most sure,
   Those vertuous habits we acquire,   90
   As being with the Soul intire,
Must with it evermore endure.

For if where sins and vice reside,
   We find so foul a guilt remain,
   As never dying in his stain,   95
Still punish'd in the Soul doth bide,

Much more that true and real joy,
   Which in a vertuous love is found,
   Must be more solid in its ground,
Then Fate or Death can e'r destroy.   100

Else should our Souls in vain elect,
   And vainer yet were Heavens laws,
   When to an everlasting Cause
They gave a perishing Effect.

Nor here on earth, then, nor above,   105
   Our good affection can impair,
   For where God doth admit the fair,
Think you that he excludeth Love?

These eyes again then, eyes shall see,
   And hands again these hands enfold,   110
   And all chast pleasures can be told
Shall with us everlasting be.

For if no use of sense remain
   When bodies once this life forsake,
   Or they could no delight partake,   115
Why should they ever rise again?

And if every imperfect mind
   Make love the end of knowledge here,
   How perfect will our love be, where
All imperfection is refin'd?   120

Let then no doubt, *Celinda,* touch,
   Much less your fairest mind invade,
   Were not our souls immortal made,
Our equal loves can make them such.

So when one wing can make no way,   125
   Two joyned can themselves dilate,

> So can two persons propagate,
> When singly either would decay.

> So when from hence we shall be gone,
>   And be no more, nor you, nor I,   130
>   As one anothers mystery,
> Each shall be both, yet both but one.

> This said, in her up-lifted face,
>   Her eyes which did that beauty crown,
>   Were like two starrs, that having faln down,   135
> Look up again to find their place:

> While such a moveless silent peace
>   Did seize on their becalmed sense,
>   One would have thought some Influence
> Their ravish'd spirits did possess.   140

For some readers, Melander's speech, which occupies the last third of the poem, may smack of a condescending instruction of the female by the more learned male, and the fact that Melander's speech is inspired by his muse, Celinda, will scarcely remove this impression. But there is a long-standing tradition in which the insight and wisdom of a woman are articulated through her role as muse. At all events, I think that Herbert treats the relationship of male to female intellect with somewhat more grace than does that far greater poet John Milton in *Paradise Lost,* where Adam reads lectures to Eve as a matter of course.

Melander begins his argument for the immortality of human love by appealing to the stars. But his address to the stars is not an empty rhetorical gesture. Melander makes clear his reason for doing so: "O you, wherein, they say, Souls rest." Moore Smith's note tells us that Plato in his *Timaeus* held that the stars are the dwelling place of souls before the souls' birth into human bodies. The stars, of course, occupied a realm considered by the ancients to be eternal, perfect, harmonious, not subject to change or decay as are all things in our sublunary world. The changeless character of the stars is, as we shall see, of the utmost importance to Melander's (and Herbert's) belief in the immortality of the soul.

Melander's speech is particularly interesting in that he makes, for an avowed Platonist, so strong a defense of the body and the senses. He does take care to distinguish between "lustful and corrupt" and "chast desires." Nevertheless, he firmly rejects any notion that we should "wholly from our thoughts exclude / Objects that may the sense delude / And study only the Divine" (lines 74–76). If we cannot fully comprehend the visible creation, Melander asks, how could we possibly comprehend the invisible? There is indeed good reason, he continues, for our study of the visible creation. Since God has expressed his greatness best in his known creatures, "Why is he not lov'd in them best?" (line 84). Celinda is thus mistaken in thinking that their love and friendship for each other will come to an end simply because these made their appearance as aspects of human life.

I read "knowledge" in line 86 as here signifying "personal acquaintance, friendship, intimacy" (*OED* 6). Shakespeare sometimes uses it thus: compare "I shall desire more love and knowledge of you" (*As You Like It,* 1.2.298).

The grammar of "But is't not true" in line 85 will puzzle the modern reader. The meaning is "But it is not true." Moore Smith cites a similar inversion in line 85 of Spenser's "October Eclogue."

In lines 94–96 Melander's argument is grounded on Plato's doctrine that soul and body so interact that a disordered soul reveals its disorder in an uncomely face and body, and a virtuous soul shines, as it were, through the face and bodily form of which it is the vital center. Melander reasons that if a man's wicked actions permanently affect the soul, then the reverse must also be true. Virtuous habits in this life become integral parts of the soul, and so come to take on the soul's immortality. Having become part of the soul, a virtuous love cannot be destroyed by death.

If, indeed, such were not the case, it would be vain for our souls to choose good rather than evil, or even to choose at all. In line 101 "elect" means "to pick out, choose (usually for a particular purpose or function)"; also as used absolutely, as here (*OED* 1).

"Impair" in line 106 is used intransitively with the meaning "to become worse, less valuable, weaker" (*OED* 2). Besides, since God manifests himself in the beautiful as well as the good and true, the presence of the beautiful ensures the presence of love as its necessary concomitant. The argument reaches its triumphant conclusion in the fine stanza that begins "These eyes again then, eyes shall see" (line 109).

In this and the following stanza Melander moves on from Platonic tradition to the specifically Christian doctrine: that God will eventually raise up the dead. With respect to the difficult lines 117–18, "And if every imperfect mind / Make love the end of knowledge here," Moore Smith calls our attention to lines 7–8 of Herbert's "Elegy for the Prince": "For what are souls but love? Since they do know / Only for it." For these lines Moore Smith supplies the following note: "This seems to go back to Plato's doctrine of knowledge, the quest of which is stimulated by Love, and the end of which is the Love of Absolute Beauty. Cf. *Symposium.*"

But one enigma here is being adduced to solve another. I simply do not understand the application of Plato's doctrine of knowledge to Herbert's "Elegy for the Prince," the opening lines of which I paraphrase thus: Why cannot we who loved the Prince restore him to life since we stored our own souls in him and death occurs only with the passage of the soul from the body. The soul, after all, is the animating force that makes the "body move."

This conceit, I grant, is strained and extravagant. But what else can the poem mean? Plato's doctrine of knowledge in any case is irrelevant to it. It also seems irrelevant to lines 66–67 of "An Ode," "And if every imperfect mind / Make love the end of knowledge here." For love in Plato's scheme is the *stimulus* for our gaining knowledge—the knowledge of Absolute Beauty, Truth, and Goodness—not the end.

I am inclined to cut the Gordian Knot by reading "knowledge" in the sense proposed above: "friendship, intimacy." To paraphrase the stanza in question: if every mind, though imperfect, makes love the ultimate goal of friendship, how perfect will that love be when the two souls aspiring to gain such a love will themselves be made perfect.

In lines 121–28, Herbert relies once more on the concept that he used in "A Meditation." A compound of elements themselves alike in their immortality will be immortal; and even if the souls of the two lovers were not in themselves immortal, their equal loves would make immortal that greater soul in which their two souls are perfectly unified. In Donne's words, quoted earlier, if "thou and I / Love so alike, that none do slacken, none can die."

Melander does not scorn to make use of analogies drawn from mortal life; one wing alone cannot fly, but two can. Two human beings can propagate and thus live on in their progeny. The next stanza (lines 129–32) continues this reference to the lovers' eventual death ("when from hence we shall be gone, / And be no more"), but the second line manifests a twist of wit. For "nor you, nor I" turns out to be not a further emphasis on the fact of their individual deaths, but introduces the theme of the greater (and deathless) soul in which they will have been united. As we read on, "nor you nor I" becomes a reference to the fact that "Each shall be both, yet both but one."

In their relation to each other they will be "one another's mystery." It is an arresting line, resonant and evocative, but just what does it mean? Melander is saying to Celinda that each will be in the other a mystical presence such as Christ is in the holy sacrament. Donne's use of "mysterious" in "The Ecstasy" ("Wee dye and rise the same, and prove / Mysterious by this love"), from which Herbert probably borrowed the notion, is not as bold as Herbert's term. For "mysterious" is more generalized and secularized—further away in derivation from its ultimately theological basis of the original sense of "mystery." The original meaning of *mystery* was "*in* or *through* [Christ's] *mystery; in* or *by* its mystical presence*" (*OED* 1a). Melander is saying that his soul's presence in Celinda's and hers in his will be analogous to Christ's mystical presence in the sacraments. Another possible analogy with another Christian doctrine is the mystery of three persons subsisting in one undivided entity as in the Holy Trinity.

With this elaboration of how two loving souls can become one greater and imperishable soul, Celinda is convinced and comforted. As they lie in each other's arms, she evidently turns her face upward to the heavens, the realm of the stars, and in lines 135–36 her eyes themselves appear to be two stars "that having faln down / Look up again to find their place," that is, their original dwelling place.

The final stanza is filled with further echoes of Donne's "Ecstasy." The spirits of the two lovers are "ravish'd"—transported, ecstatic. They experience a "moveless silent peace"; their senses have not been denied them but are now "becalmed." But "silent" and "moveless" also suggest once more the realm of the fixed stars, where there is no noise, no change, no decay, no disharmony. The lovers' ravishment is indeed an effect of the influence of the stars. The poet, it is true, says no more than "One would have thought some Influence / [The lovers'] ravish'd spirits did possess." But Herbert's seventeenth-century reader would not have had to be told from where that influence came. The term has been traced as far back as the late Latin *influxus* (*stellarum*): "astral influence . . . was common in medieval Latin" and was common in the Renaissance (*OED*).

In "L'Allegro" Milton obviously uses influence in this sense and, like Herbert, is associating eyes with stars: "With more of Ladies, whose bright eies / Rain influence, and judge the prise." "Her eyes were like stars," that oldest and already by Herbert's time most badly worn of similes, is brought back into vital metaphoric life in such passages as Milton's and Herbert's.

As for "An Ode," from the moment when Melander addresses the stars (line 65) until the last stanza, the stars dominate the poem. They denote the timeless, peaceful, and immortal. They are the soul's origin, and they point back to its final abode.

VII

Love, Time, and Eternity

Andrew Marvell

To his Coy Mistress

Had we but World enough, and Time,
This coyness Lady were no crime.
We would sit down, and think which way
To walk, and pass our long Loves Day.
Thou by the *Indian Ganges* side   5
Should'st Rubies find: I by the Tide
Of *Humber* would complain. I would
Love you ten years before the Flood:
And you should, if you please, refuse
Till the Conversion of the *Jews*.   10
My vegetable Love should grow
Vaster than Empires, and more slow.
An hundred years should go to praise
Thine Eyes, and on thy Forehead Gaze.
Two hundred to adore each Breast: 15
But thirty thousand to the rest.
An Age at least to every part,
And the last Age should show your Heart.
For Lady you deserve this State;
Nor would I love at lower rate.   20
    But at my back I alwaies hear
Times winged Charriot hurrying near:
And yonder all before us lye
Deserts of vast Eternity.
Thy Beauty shall no more be found;   25
Nor, in thy marble Vault, shall sound
My ecchoing Song: then Worms shall try
That long preserv'd Virginity:
And your quaint Honour turn to dust;

And into ashes all my Lust.   30
The Grave's a fine and private place,
But none I think do there embrace.
    Now therefore, while the youthful hew
Sits on thy skin like morning glew,
And while thy willing Soul transpires   35
At every pore with instant Fires,
Now let us sport us while we may;
And now, like am'rous birds of prey,
Rather at once our Time devour,
Than languish in his slow-chapt pow'r.   40
Let us roll all our Strength, and all
Our sweetness, up into one Ball:
And tear our Pleasures with rough strife,
Thorough the Iron gates of Life:
Thus, though we cannot make our Sun   45
Stand still, yet we will make him run.

The Garden

i

How vainly men themselves amaze
To win the Palm, the Oke, or Bayes;
And their uncessant Labours see
Crown'd from some single Herb or Tree,
Whose short and narrow verged Shade   5
Does prudently their Toyles upbraid;
While all Flow'rs and all Trees do close
To weave the Garlands of repose.

ii

Fair quiet, have I found thee here,
And Innocence thy Sister dear!   10
Mistaken long, I sought you then
In busie Companies of Men.
Your sacred Plants, if here below,
Only among the Plants will grow.
Society is all but rude,   15
To this delicious Solitude.

iii

No white nor red was ever seen
So am'rous as this lovely green.
Fond Lovers, cruel as their Flame,

Cut in these Trees their Mistress name.   20
Little, Alas, they know, or heed,
How far these Beauties Hers exceed!
Fair Trees! where s'ere your barkes I wound,
No Name shall but your own be found.

iv
When we have run our Passions heat,   25
Love hither makes his best retreat.
The *Gods,* that mortal Beauty chase,
Still in a Tree did end their race.
Apollo hunted *Daphne* so,
Only that She might Laurel grow.   30
And *Pan* did after *Syrinx* speed,
Not as a Nymph, but for a Reed.

v
What wond'rous Life in this I lead!
Ripe Apples drop about my head;
The Luscious Clusters of the Vine   35
Upon my Mouth do crush their Wine;
The Nectaren, and curious Peach,
Into my hands themselves do reach;
Stumbling on Melons, as I pass,
Insnar'd with Flow'rs, I fall on Grass.   40

vi
Mean while the Mind, from pleasures less,
Withdraws into its happiness:
The Mind, that Ocean where each kind
Does streight its own resemblance find;
Yet it creates, transcending these,   45
Far other Worlds, and other Seas;
Annihilating all that's made
To a green Thought in a green Shade.

vii
Here at the Fountains sliding foot,
Or at some Fruit-tree's mossy root,   50
Casting the Bodies Vest aside,
My Soul into the boughs does glide:
There like a Bird it sits, and sings,
Then whets, and combs its silver Wings;
And, till prepar'd for longer flight,   55
Waves in its Plumes the various Light.

viii
Such was that happy Garden-state,
While Man there walk'd without a Mate:
After a Place so pure, and sweet,
What other Help could yet be meet!   60
But 'twas beyond a Mortal's share
To wander solitary there:
Two Paradises 'twere in one
To live in Paradise alone.

ix
How well the skilful Gardner drew   65
Of flow'rs and herbes this Dial new;
Where from above the milder Sun
Does through a fragrant Zodiack run;
And, as it works, th' industrious Bee
Computes its time as well as we.   70
How could such sweet and wholsome Hours
Be reckon'd but with herbs and flow'rs!

Andrew Marvell's "The Garden" and "To His Coy Mistress" are, by common consent I should think, two of the finest lyric poems in English. Yet "The Garden" would seem to abjure altogether sexual love, whereas "To His Coy Mistress" is one of the most powerful of all such appeals to enjoy love while youth lasts. Now, sane readers do not regard poems, either lyric or dramatic, as necessarily declarations of personal faith, duly attested and sworn to by the author. Poets have a right—although one not always respected by literary critics—to adopt differing and even contradictory premises on which to base their poems.

Nevertheless, the clash between the world views involved in "The Garden" and "To His Coy Mistress" is calculated to bring up once more that perennial concern with the poet's sincerity. Thus, one may want to ask which of the two poems really represents what Marvell, the man, felt and believed. After all, "To His Coy Mistress" carries so much conviction that it is difficult to dismiss it as simply an exercise. Some of Marvell's other carpe diem poems, of course, do read like mere exercises—his "Daphne and Chloe," for example.

Biographical considerations may complicate the issue. Marvell's known Puritan leanings suggest to many readers that such poems as "The Garden" must surely represent Marvell's real convictions; and perhaps they do. But, interested as all of us must be in Andrew Marvell the man, I shall be concerned here primarily with what gives these poems their force and sense of conviction, and what accounts for their grace and seeming inevitability as dramatic statements.

Moreover, the way readers remember prior assumptions about the author's mind and character may actually distort the poem.[1] The relation between the poet and his work is obviously intimate and intricate. We may properly look to the poem for a reflection of, or perhaps better, a selection from, the poet's attitudes, values, and ideas, for poets write out of different moods and out of different situations, real or imagined. "To His Coy Mistress" was certainly a product of Marvell's shaping imagination, but so was "The Garden."

What these two poems say and are has been thoroughly canvassed during the last several decades. We possess, therefore, a rich and detailed account of the classical background of the poems, the various literary sources upon which Marvell drew or might have drawn, and the analogues to be found in other poets of the Renaissance, both Marvell's predecessors and his contemporaries. I shall have little here to add to this sort of important information. In any case, I mean to concern myself with two rather different matters: the dramatic and tonal structure of these poems and the parallels and contrasts that exist between them.

For all their apparent oppositions and contradictions, the poems have much in common. They share several themes, one of which I believe has received less attention than it deserves: the theme of time in relation to eternity. I suggest that we try to imagine the lover of "To His Coy Mistress" to be the same man who steps into "The Garden" and savors its cool delights. Let's imagine that he has been unable to persuade his coy mistress to yield her body to him. Now, after the failure of his plea, he has found in this delightful place "love['s] . . . best retreat." Nature proves to be no coy mistress, but offers her innocent pleasures wholeheartedly.

Professor Gregory Vlastos, after reading an earlier draft of this essay, remarked to me that the reference in "The Garden" to one's having run through his "Passions heat" could suggest a very different interpretation; that if we are to imagine the speaker of "To His Coy Mistress" to be also the speaker of "The Garden," we might also imagine that his coy mistress, rather than denying her importunate lover, has yielded herself. I found I had to agree with Vlastos that the latter supposition will serve

---

1. See, for example, Pierre Legouis's account of "The Coronet" on pp. 87–88 of his impressively learned *Andrew Marvell: Poet, Puritan, Patriot.*

very well to account for the lover's thoughts in the garden. That very fact may tell us something about the relationship of the two poems to each other.

The lover, whether we imagine him as denied or satisfied, might well find the "lovely green" of nature more "am'rous" than the "white" and "red" of the mistress from whom he had departed an hour before. Yet what about the phrase *vegetable love,* which he had earlier used contemptuously to dismiss a love affair that had little to recommend it except the long life and slow growth characteristic of a plant? If the "Fair Trees" of the garden are indeed more amorously attractive than any woman, does not their love also have to be regarded as a "vegetable love"?

In view of such problems, we may want to dismiss as simply unprofitable the little fantasy that I have proposed. Yet I hope the reader can be persuaded to indulge it a little further in the possibility that it might, after all, throw a ray of light on both poems: in particular, light on how much each poem depends on a given dramatic situation, on the mood of the character speaking the poem, and on the tone in which he makes his various utterances.

Let me begin, however, with the theme of time and mortality. The lover of the coy mistress never for a moment relaxes his concern with the swift rush of time. His imagery in the first third of the poem does seem to slow the passage of time as he describes the most protracted of courtships. His account is studded with references to events in the far-off past, such as Noah's Flood, or events that are to occur only in some very remote future, such as the Conversion of the Jews. (One notes that though the lover seems to be something of a libertine, he is clearly familiar with the Holy Scriptures.)

All this witty hyperbole is meant, of course, to render preposterous so slow-paced a courtship and to prepare for the sudden speedup of time found in the middle third of the poem—a rush that will soon take the lovers out of life altogether and strand their bodies in "Deserts of vast Eternity." The tone of the whole section is ironic and almost brutally realistic. Consider the phrase *quaint Honour.* Here *quaint* must signify something "Dainty, fastidious, nice, prim" (*OED* 10). Yet "quaint Honour" for the seventeenth-century audience may well have carried a direct reference to the girl's sexuality. At that time *honour* often was used with special reference to a woman's chastity "as a virtue of the highest consideration" (*OED* 3), and it sometimes was used to refer specifically to the female genitalia (*OED* 3b). Furthermore, such an inference would be strengthened by the fact that *quaint* as a noun was also sometimes used to refer to the female genitalia. (*OED* cites such a reference as late as 1598.) The poet found in "quaint Honour" a phrase very rich in suggestions apt to his purpose here.

The strategy, of course, is to present with laconic irony a bleak reality which exposes the earlier fantasy for the ridiculous posturing that it is. Having done so, the lover is ready to urge his conclusion: since there is no way to arrest time or even slow it—after all, the lovers cannot, like Joshua, command the sun to stand still—the only course is to beat time at time's own game, to live with such breathless speed as to cause the sun, which makes and marks the passage of time, to lag behind them. Thus, a concern with time dominates the whole poem.

Though a reference to speed—that of the lovers' outracing the sun—occupies the final couplet, the dominant image of the closing lines of the poem is one of eating. The lovers are to devour their pleasures greedily. Far from being the lovebirds of tradition, turtledoves billing and cooing, they are conceived as "am'rous birds of prey"—a pair of hunting hawks, snatching and tearing at the flesh of a rabbit or bird. Time also is a devourer, but his inevitable jaws are slow, as he gradually masticates all mortal things. This figure has its exactness. Hawks, of course, do not chew their food; they tear the flesh to pieces and bolt it down. Marvell's is not a pretty picture, this scene of ravenous gluttony. But then the poet does not want a dainty picture here. He has used this figure deliberately. He even calls the lovers' activity a "rough strife."

The Folio of 1681 reads, for line 44, "Thorough the Iron gates of Life." For generations this was the accepted text—in fact the only text we had—and there have been a great many conjectures as to what were those gates through which the lovers were exhorted to tear their pleasures. Some of them have been preposterous. Elizabeth Story Donno in her Penguin edition of Marvell's poetry mentions "the reach of the Danube" (Margoliouth) and metaphoric *labia* (Dennis Davison)."[2]

Professor Donno follows the Popple manuscript corrections to the Folio and reads "iron grates." I accept "grates" as probably the correct reading. The Popple manuscript, long lost, came to light and was acquired by the Bodleian Library in 1944. Yet before I even knew of the Popple manuscript the image always brought to my mind by lines 43–44 was of a pair of hawks mewed up in an iron cage. They will not wait for their keeper to poke through the bars the raw meat on which they are

2. Elizabeth Story Donno, ed., *Andrew Marvell: The Complete Poems,* 235.

fed, but snatch at it with their beaks and pull it through. I am therefore gratified that we now have textual authority for "grates," and I note that *grate* in the seventeenth century could signify a barred cage. (See *OED* 7: "A barred place of confinement for animals, also a prison or cage for human beings.) Some of the illustrative passages cited by the *OED* are interesting: 1613, "Lions and Leopards in grates"; 1759, "He was now as impatient as an eagle in a grate." The image of ravenous birds tearing their food between them provides a sense of creatures savage and uninhibited and admirably accords with the conclusion of the poem. For the mood of the poem is vehement and charged with urgency.

Though the images that occur in these concluding lines (38–46) may seem loose and random, there is in fact a definite chain of association. The rapid beaks of birds that can scarcely wait for their food are set off against Time's slow-moving jaws. The hawks are caged, but all creatures are imprisoned in mortality and live under sentence of death. (In his "Dialogue between the Soul and Body," Marvell describes man's soul as imprisoned in the body: "With bolts of Bones, that fetter'd stands / In Feet, and manacled in Hands.") Why should the lovers not imitate those amorous birds of prey and, instead of languishing in time's prison to await being devoured, eagerly devour what they can while they can? In the concluding couplet the image shifts, but the appeal for dynamic action continues. Rather than wait resignedly for the sun to set on their "long Loves Day" (line 4), better to try to outrun the sun itself.

The use of this series of images represents one way in which "To His Coy Mistress" differs from most of the carpe diem poems of this period. Another way is the insistence on the grimly physical. Marvell stresses the corrupting corpse and the grave-worm. It is true enough that Marvell's worm is not the never-dying worm of the Scriptures, cited by generations of hellfire preachers. Marvell's is a quite matter-of-fact worm, doing what he may be expected to do to all mortal flesh. Yet, if one is to look for any trace of Marvell's Puritanism, I think that it might be found here. The note of grim horror introduced sets up a reverberation that is deeper and more powerful than is to be heard in any other carpe diem poem that I can think of. Compare it with the Anglican Herrick's masterpiece, "Corinna's Going a-Maying." Marvell's poem is not necessarily "better," but it is certainly of another order.

To most readers, the voice heard in this poem is not, of course, that of a Puritan but that of a seventeenth-century libertine, someone, say, like the earl of Rochester. Yet the Puritan and the libertine may be more closely allied than we are in the habit of supposing. After all, the libertine of Marvell's day was not a pagan suckled in a creed outworn. He had almost certainly been brought up on the Ten Commandments and the Apostle's Creed. In short, he was typically a lapsed Christian, whether now cynical about, indifferent to, or defiant of, his heritage. Yet it has been difficult for him to expunge completely that which he had been brought up to believe and to which his society still gave more than lip service.

As I have already hinted, the general tone of Marvell's poem is surely not precisely classical. When Catullus reminds his Lesbia that both will eventually have to descend into everlasting night, the note sounded is quite different. *Nox est perpetua una dormienda* is sufficiently somber to give urgency to his plea that Lesbia give him her love while she may. But Catullus's description of that perpetual night as one in which one must sleep forever mitigates something of its horror. He does not mention the grave-worm.

J. B. Leishman has pointed out an analogy and a possible source of Marvell's poem in an epigram by Asclepiades in the *Greek Anthology*, which he translates, "Hoarding your maidenhood—and why? For not when to Hades you've gone down shall you find, maiden, the lover you lack. Only among the alive are the joys of Cypris, and only, maiden, as bones and dust shall we in Acheron lie." In spirit this poem is closer to Catullus than to Marvell's poem; even so, it has neither the urgency nor the grim irony of "To His Coy Mistress."

In sum, the lover of "To His Coy Mistress," in spite of his brilliant rhetoric, high-flown compliment, urbanity, and grace, impresses me, I repeat, as a desperate man, though his is a desperation held under firm control.

Time is a basic concern in "The Garden" as well as in "To His Coy Mistress." The man whose thoughts constitute the poem is very much conscious of time, even though, in this poem, he is stepping into the garden and out of the hurrying blast of time. The poem begins on a note of surprise, a happy surprise at what the speaker has just discovered when he enters the garden precincts: Quiet and Innocence. Clearly, he has heretofore failed to find them in the "busie Companies of Men," or, as stanzas 3 and 4 indicate, in the society of women, with whom he associates the inevitable disappointments of love. His discovery of Quiet and Innocence is as surprising to him as it is welcome. How else account for lines such as "Fair quiet, have I found thee here, / And Innocence thy Sister dear." The note is one of joyful relief.

To assess correctly the dramatic situation out of which the garden meditation arises—whether or not we indulge the fancy that the man speaking is the lover of "To His Coy Mistress"—will allow us to take in the proper spirit the teasing of the ladies that occupies stanzas 3 and 4. A quite liberal reading would make the speaker a misogynist or at least a very sour Puritan. Though he is here sardonic about romantic love, this disillusioned lover is not a man with a settled dislike for females.

The speaker's praise of the beauty of the world of trees and plants to the disparagement of the beauty of woman brings up once more the subject of "vegetable Love." Some commentators on "To His Coy Mistress" have been apprehensive that "vegetable Love" might make the modern reader envisage a cabbage or a carrot—Gilbert and Sullivan's Bunthorne, one remembers, pretended to a "passion of a vegetable fashion" and meditates on a dalliance with a "not too French French bean." These commentators have taken pains to point out that Marvell's use here refers only to such an entity as possessed merely the "vegetative soul," the vital principle of the plant world. In the old hierarchy of souls, the next highest was the "animal soul," the animating principle of animal life. Man alone possessed the highest in the hierarchy, a "rational soul."

This is all true enough, but the concession hardly diminishes the disparagement contained in the phrase *vegetable Love*. For things animated by no more than a vegetative soul constitute the very lowest ebb of living nature. The lover speaking to his coy mistress is properly contemptuous of a love that, like a plant, even a centuries-old yew tree, can do little more than keep growing and propagating itself. He asks for a love that has fire and passion.

In view of all this, what does one make of the love for trees, fruit, and flowers professed in "The Garden"? How seriously—even setting aside the mocking reference to "vegetable Love" in "To His Coy Mistress"— can we accept such an assertion?

Obviously, the tone in which the professions are made and the dramatic situation that elicits them are all-important here. If we want to indulge a little further the supposition that the person speaking to his coy mistress is the person now reveling in the garden, we could say that after having failed to convince his mistress, he is now in the garden venting his pique at her and at women in general. In any case, his ironic assessment of the conventional tribute to their beauty, it would seem clear, does not come from someone constitutionally indifferent to women or from a mere novice at the game of love. This railer against women is very likely one of the "Fond Lovers" at whose folly he now smiles. The voice we hear surely comes out of experience, not ignorance.

Yet whether or not we refuse to indulge the fancy that our poems are spoken by one man who is speaking out of two contrasting moods, there is in "The Garden" itself plenty of evidence that his praise of nature's peace and quiet is more than a mere spiteful revulsion from an unrequited or fulfilled and disappointing love. It springs from genuine joy. For to this speaker, nature is not only delightful in itself, but points to delights beyond itself. It hints of a peace and innocence that transcend the mortal world.

In "The Garden," then, the attraction of those things animated only by the vegetative soul can speak to the rational soul of a contemplative man. The animal soul in this poem, by the way, receives little emphasis. In "To His Coy Mistress," of course, the animal soul very properly gets primary emphasis—clearly so in the powerful image of the greedy feasting of the pair of "am'rous birds of prey." "To His Coy Mistress" does provide an answer to mortal man under the threat of time. But a very different answer is provided by the reference to the bird with "silver Wings" that in "The Garden" prepares itself "for longer flight."

In "The Garden," as in "To His Coy Mistress," Marvell's control of tone is masterly. In the latter poem, the movement is from rather good-humored hyperbole, through a biting, sardonic wit, back to hyperbole again, but this time at once defiant and exultant. The shifts in tone are appropriate to, and help define, the three parts of the syllogistic structure of the poem. In the more complex structure of "The Garden," the tonal shifts are more subtle and more intricate.

In "The Garden" the attitude shifts from amused reflection on the folly and self-deception of men to happy surprise and glad relief at discovering—almost accidentally?—the true abode of quiet and innocence. His delight moves the speaker toward a witty and high-spirited praise of the plants and trees, and mockery of the conventional claims for female beauty. With a learned mock-seriousness, the poet brazens out his case with proofs fabricated by a reinterpretation of two classical myths.

With stanza 5, he gives himself up to the fruits and flowers of the garden's little paradise. He compares his "wondrous Life" to that led by an as yet sinless and solitary Adam during the first hours of his existence in an Eve-less Eden. A brave new world, indeed, made its impact on the first man's unjaded senses. It was a world to be explored with rapture by one wholly free of any distraction—even the distraction provided by a companion and mate.

Nature is here regarded as a completely yielding mistress. Her fruits and flowers offer themselves without hesitation or reservation. The vines press their grape clusters into his mouth. The melons before his feet seem to strive to make him stumble, and the very flowers ensnare him and pull him down upon the earth. *Stumble, ensnare,* and *fall* are loaded terms in the Christian vocabulary. The words suggest seduction by sensual pleasures and a fall from grace; and indeed, the speaker soon becomes, like Adam, literally a fallen man. But nature's embrace is innocent. There are no broken vows, jealousies, or aftermaths of remorse. (In stanza 8 the poet will develop this hint of the Eden story into an explicit reference.)

Yet, though Marvell has deliberately invoked sexual overtones in describing the reception that Nature affords this grateful recipient of peace, he never relaxes his grasp upon common sense and reality. The man in the garden has given himself up wholly to the garden's cool shade because it offers a blessed respite from the burden and heat of a day within a too busy life. But we may be sure that he will not try to overstay his hour or so of bliss. The poem is no manifesto for primitivism. The man who experienced it has not resolved to live for the rest of his life in solitude as a hermit in some wilderness. He does not even suggest an anticipation of William Wordsworth.

The conception of nature implied in "The Garden" seems to me thoroughly orthodox. Nature is indeed innocent. In this poem it is not Plato's lower and grosser element on which the divine forms can only imperfectly make their imprint. It is certainly not the Manichaean's actively evil force at war with the good. The natural world has been created good by a good Creator. It has not brought about man's Fall. Man has only himself to blame for that. Having in mind the possible influence of Puritanism on his poetry, we can say that on this particular issue Marvell is as orthodox as that other great Puritan, his friend, the John Milton of *Paradise Lost.* Neither poet holds nature in contempt.

Marvell does indeed regard the felicities that nature offers as lower than those available to the soul. See his "A Dialogue Between the Resolved Soul, and Created Pleasure," "On a Drop of Dew," "Clorinda and Damon," "Thyrsis and Dorinda," and "A Dialogue Between the Soul and Body." Yet one notices that in this last-named poem the poet allows the Body the final word—and what a telling word it is. The Body argues that it is not the Body that corrupts the Soul, but the Soul the Body:

> What but a Soul could have the wit
> To build me up for Sin so fit?
> So Architects do square and hew
> Green Trees that in the Forest grew.

The Body, like the trees praised in "The Garden" for their "lovely green," would, left to itself, fulfill its own possibilities, instinctively and innocently. It is the "Tyrannic Soul" that frustrates and tortures it.

One learns to respect the solid intellectual and theological base that undergirds nearly all of Marvell's poems. That the poems are so based has much to do with their structural coherence, which furnishes the grounding for the pointed applications of Marvell's serious wit. One might observe that even "To His Coy Mistress" can be fitted onto this same theological base. For if one puts the highest valuation on the pleasures of the body, then one had indeed better seize the day and enjoy its pleasures now. They perish with the perishing of the body. One would be foolish to expect them in the Christian afterlife, for the Scriptures are very specific on this point: in the Christian heaven there is no marriage or giving in marriage. If one does not believe in an afterlife, or, though believing, sets his highest value on the fulfillment of his bodily desires, then the argument made to the coy mistress is perfectly sound.

The best evidence that the speaker regards the pleasures of nature as in themselves innocent is to be found in stanza 6, where the body's delight in nature does not distract the rational soul from its higher pleasure. Indeed, it is when the body is appeased and innocently happy that the mind can "Withdraw into its happiness" (line 43). This pleasure peculiar to the rational soul points toward a transcendence that is fully developed in the final stanzas of the poem. The garden's quiet joys allow the contemplative man to become for a moment a disembodied soul and to gain some sense of what the joyful freedom of pure spirit would be.

Yet how skillfully Marvell manages the tone here. Instead of the high spirits and hyperbole of some of the earlier stanzas or the ironic teasing in still others, in stanza 7 he is precise, restrained, careful not to overstate. Thus, the soul, like an uncaged bird, flies only a little way from the body—goes no further than a nearby bough, where "like a Bird it sits, and sings, / Then whets, and combs its silver Wings" (lines 53–54). The image is beautifully apt: it suggests the soul's timidity at finding itself outside its familiar habitation, the joy that makes it sing, and its almost childlike pleasure in the discovery that it has silver wings, wings that it now preens in a sort of innocent vanity.

Stanza 8 provides a nice example of Marvell's classic restraint. Even at this high point of the experience, the metaphor used makes very moderate claims. The soul is allowed no more than a glimpse of its future bliss. It dare not presume on its spiritual powers. The poet is even very practical in justifying the soul's actions in spreading its wings. It is well for it now to prepare for the "longer flight" that some day, permanently separated from the body, it must take.

Marvell observes here, as in so much of his poetry, Horace's dictum that there is a proper measure in all things. When he does exaggerate, he does it so thoroughly that we are never in doubt as to how seriously to take him. He sometimes employs witty hyperbole or, as Leishman somewhere puts it, sometimes mere "waggishness." Yet when Marvell is thoroughly serious, his assertions are moderate and credible.

The method shows itself in the structure of the closing stanzas of the poem. After touching briefly on the ecstasy of the momentarily disembodied soul, the next stanza (8) resumes the banter we have heard earlier. Just as in stanza 4 Marvell has perversely inverted the classic myths of Apollo's pursuit of Daphne and Pan's pursuit of Syrinx, in stanza 8 he proceeds to turn upside down the Biblical account of the creation of Eve. He insists that God gave Eve to Adam not because he needed a help meet (suitable) for him but because God regarded his delicious solitude as entirely too good for a mere mortal to enjoy (as if Marvell did not well know that Adam did not become mortal until *after* the creation of Eve and the breaking of God's express command, the act that brought death into the world and all our woe). But Marvell is quite cheerful in his irreverence. He can hardly be trying to delude his readers, saturated as he knew them to be in the Scriptures. So much for his waggishness in introducing a transparently specious bit of evidence to strengthen his case for the delights of solitude.

In the next and final stanza of the poem, however, classic moderation again reasserts itself. If the poet is playful in proposing that "'twas beyond a Mortal's share" to live alone in the earthly paradise, he is very properly serious in implying, as the poem closes, that it is indeed beyond any mortal's share to live *continually* in the full light of eternity. For if one could do that, he would have ceased to be mortal.

"The Garden," one repeats, is the meditation of a man who respects the limitations of his mortality. The speaker's meditation on the garden's delights has by now clearly reentered the world of time. How do we know this? Well, among other things, because of the reference to the sundial in the final stanza. The numerals of this dial consist of artfully shaped beds of flowers. Such a chronometer is, of course, thoroughly appropriate to the garden. Nevertheless, it *is* a timepiece, and it reminds us that time has never stopped its motion even during an experience which has seemed a blessed respite from time. The sun has not stopped still; there has been some movement of the shadow around the dial.

Though the poet amusingly fancies that the "industrious" bee is consulting the clock for the time of day, it is actually gathering nectar and pollen from the flowers. The sun duly moves through his twelve signs ("fragrant Zodiak") of the dial just as he moves through the heavenly zodiac in the course that makes up the year.

Though time, in this floral sundial, does seem slowed and gentled, almost tamed, the fact of time—winged chariot or no—is acknowledged. Mortal man can escape from time only in brief and blessed intervals, and even those escapes from time are finally illusory except as they may possibly point to some future state. But to the contemplative man depicted in the poem, time is not terrifying, for here time does not eventually lose itself in the vast deserts of eternity. There waits beyond time an eternity in a realm of joy that no earthly garden can do more than foreshadow.

"To His Coy Mistress" and "The Garden" are remarkable poems, but it is not remarkable that one and the same poet could write them. They do reflect, to be sure, differing views of time and eternity, but they have much in common in the ideas they touch upon. In any case, they are not declarations of faith but presentations of two differing world views, dramatizations made by a poet who, though suffused with the Christian concept of reality and the ethic it implies, also knew his classics well and had evidently read them with sympathy.

Like a great many men of his era, Marvell was concerned to incorporate into the Christian scheme as much as possible of the classical insights and wisdom. But, when he chose, he could also treat with understanding and at least dramatic sympathy the great classical literary forms, not only as frames of reference, but as representing time-honored classical attitudes toward life and death. He makes such a presentation in "To His Coy Mistress." But as I have suggested earlier, it may be possible to find even in this pagan-classical poem a trace of Christian and even Puritan feeling, particularly in the references to death. After all, Marvell had not lived in the happy pagan time in which, as Théophile Gautier conceived it, the skeleton was kept invisible. Like John Webster, Marvell "saw the skull beneath the skin." Yet, whatever its source, such a Christian alloy serves to harden the softer classical metal with a touch of medieval horror. It adds force to the argument of the poem and gives the argument a sharper cutting edge.

To sum up, on the evidence of the two poems we have been comparing, Marvell was not a man who was unable to make up his mind or a waverer between commitments or a trimmer. A comparison of the poems tells quite another story: it reveals the presence of fair-mindedness, awareness of alternatives, and sensitivity to the complexity of the issues involved.

The evidence to be gathered from Marvell's life is, I believe, in general conformity with such a view, but Marvell's character as a man, I repeat, is not the matter of my special concern in this essay. The matter of concern is the kind of mind and sensibility reflected in his lyrical poems.

It is essentially the mind of the late Renaissance at its best. This poet is learned. He is thoroughly at home with the earlier literature of the West. He is familiar with classical philosophy as well as Christian theology. He regards both as constituting a valuable inheritance. His aim is to assimilate their lore and to develop, as far as possible, a synthesis that will take the whole past into account.

Yet the weight of knowledge has not burdened and so made heavy and slow the poet's sensibility. He does not take himself too seriously. He observes a sense of proportion. He can, on occasion, exaggerate, be playful, and speak in hyperbole. But his wit can modulate into the deepest seriousness. Marvell's admirers have oftentimes stressed his restraint, his moderation, his dispassionate stance, and such terms surely have their truth. But they do not tell the whole truth about this poet's mind and spirit, and they can be misunderstood. Thus, his dispassionate judgment does not mean that his poems lack passion. "To His Coy Mistress" is a passionate poem. So, in a very different way, is "The Garden"; and so, for that matter, is "A Dialogue Between the Soul and Body." Again, "restraint" and "moderation" must not be taken to mean lack of power. In Marvell, power is present, but controlled and directed to an end.

I would like to suggest some alternate way of describing the mind and sensibility that one finds expressed in his poetry. One has to say mind *and* sensibility, for in his best poetry they are so thoroughly engaged that they can scarcely be discussed apart. And why should they be? In a healthy society and in a healthy literature they interact. Marvell's serious wit is essentially the intelligence enlisted in the service of the whole personality, and that is as it should be. One can use other terms still: one can say that the imagination, with its concern for images, bodies forth the conceptions of the intellect. Marvell is a master at controlling this interaction and effecting a true synthesis of the personality.

In saying this, I have, of course, simply repeated once more the often asserted claims for metaphysical poetry. But how can one avoid doing so if one is to talk about the sensibility revealed in Marvell's characteristic poems? How else, indeed, since those poems in my opinion are perhaps the purest examples of the essential qualities of metaphysical poetry. Mind you, I say the purest, not necessarily the most exciting or engaging, or even the most valuable. But for Marvell to have expressed this synthesizing power in perhaps its purest form is a sufficient tribute to his genius.

To look at his poetry in this way is perhaps the best way to account for an ultimate seriousness tempered by a graceful urbanity, a quality that sets Marvell apart from the overconfident or the single-minded man, and even from the victim of a temporary enthusiasm—a quality that betokens a fine sanity and a wonderfully uncommon common sense.

A note on the text of "To His Coy Mistress"

The Popple manuscript of Marvell's poems is so important that the reader will allow this note to be worth his trouble. In her text of this poem, Professor Donno prints lines 33–34 as follows:

> Now, therefore, while the youthful glue
> Sits on thy skin like morning dew.

She is following the reading in the Popple manuscript, except that the manuscript uses the spelling *glew*. The 1681 Folio reads:

> Now therefore, while the youthful hew
> Sits on thy skin like morning glew.

A primary problem is the occurrence in both texts of "glew." Professor Donno obviously takes the word to mean an adhesive substance and so modernizes the spelling to "glue." She writes that "the sense of *youthful glue* is entirely consonant with the theme of the poem" and that the following quotation makes this clear: "'Life is nothing else but as it were a glue, which in man fasteneth the soul and body together.' William Baldwin, Moral Philosophy, 1547. Cited in the *OED*."

If, however, "youthful glue" means youthful *life,* would the poet say that it "sits" on a young woman's skin, or that it looks like "morning dew"? I doubt it. In earlier ages it was the heart that was regarded as the dwelling place of the animating principle.

One does not have to quarrel here with the authority of the Popple manuscript—which is great—in order to object to "glue." My concern is with what precisely Marvell meant when he wrote "glew."

Some years ago I took this matter up with the late Helge Kökeritz, whose special province was the history of the English language. Remembering that Marvell was a Yorkshireman, I asked him whether *glew* might, in the seventeenth-century Yorkshire dialect, be a variant of *glow.* He provided me with the following note.

> *Glew*
>
> The normal development of OE ō + *w* as in OE *glōwan* was to ME *o̜u,* thus ME *glo̜wen;* in other words, OE *o̜w* coalesced with the descendant of OE *āw,* giving modern [ou] (cf. Jordan-Matthes, *Handbuch der mittelenglischen Grammatik*). But in the northern English dialects ME *o̜* < OE *ō,* whether followed by *w* or not, developed differently. It became a fronted sound, [ü:], variously written *u, ew* (Jordan-Matthes §54, §119). Here, therefore, OE *ōw* would become *uw, ew,* etc., reflected in such ME spellings as *stue, stywe, stew* (14th c., NED, *stow* v.1). There seems to be no trace of this development at all in the modern northern dialects, which have apparently adopted (and modified) the southern English diphthong ou. Doubtless, however, a vowel or diphthong, spelled *ew* and capable of rhyming with *ue* in *hue,* existed in the earlier periods of these northern dialects. Marvell's *glew* must consequently be a dialectal form of *glow.* For the development of northern ME *o̜* see also H. Orton, *Englische Studien* 63, pp. 229–251 (The Medial Development of ME $\bar{o}_1$ (tense) etc.)

Consider the alternatives to reading Marvell's "glew" as a dialectical form of glow. The glues available in the seventeenth century, and for long afterward, were derived from the hides, hooves, skins, and bones of animals. They were not colorless like dew and were definitely sticky and often smelly. Birdlime was an obviously gooey glue. The unattractiveness of a skin covered with drops or smears of glue can be judged by a remark made by one of Ben Jonson's characters in *Every Man Out of His Humor* (5.4): "I think that thou dost Varnish thy face with the fat on't, it looks so like a Glew-pot."

If it be objected, however, that the form *glew* in the Folio was also accepted by William Popple, Marvell's favorite nephew, who corrected the Folio text in manuscript, the answer would have to be that Popple was himself almost certainly a Yorkshireman and spoke his uncle's dialect. (Such Popples as I have been able to locate in this period were all Yorkshiremen.)

If Marvell's meaning was really "morning glow," the suitor's compliment to his mistress would make perfect sense. The complexion of a young woman was often compared to the warm blush of the sky at dawn. *Glow* means "brightness and warmth of color."

Moreover, if we are to take seriously the impact of the lines that follow, "And while thy willing soul transpires / At every pore with instant fires," surely no viscous liquid like glue could be imagined to exude from a lovely woman's skin. What is breathed out from the soul, that "fiery particle," would be warmth and brightness.

I would go further still. I can't believe that even a liquid as innocent as dew sat upon the coy mistress's skin. She was not perspiring from having just completed the hundred-yard dash. Such drops as, for instance, Herrick's Corinna wears are drops of dew shaken from the trees under which she passes. I prefer to drop the reference to "dew" altogether and to retain the Folio text.

VIII

A Pre-Romantic View of Nature ☿

Sir Richard Lovelace

The Grasse-Hopper

To my Noble Friend, Mr. Charles Cotton.
Ode

I
Oh thou that swing'st upon the waving haire
   Of some well-filled Oaten Beard,
Drunke ev'ry night with a Delicious teare
   Dropt thee from Heav'n, where now th'art reard.
II
The Joyes of Earth and Ayre are thine intire,   5
   That with thy feet and wings dost hop and flye;
And when thy Poppy workes thou dost retire
   to thy Carv'd Acron-bed to lye.
III
Up with the Day, thy Sun thou welcomst then,
   Sportst in the guilt-plats of his Beames,   10
And all these merry dayes mak'st merry men,
   Thy selfe, and Melancholy streames.
IV
But ah the Sickle! Golden Eares are Cropt;
   Ceres and Bacchus bid good night;
Sharpe frosty fingers all your Flowr's have topt,   15
   And what sithes spar'd, Winds shave off quite.
V
Poore verdant foole! and now green Ice! thy Joys
   Large and as lasting, as thy Peirch of Grasse,
Bid us lay in 'gainst Winter, Raine, and poize
   Their flouds, with an o'reflowing glasse.   20
VI
Thou best of *Men* and *Friends*! we will create

A Genuine Summer in each others breast;
And spite of this cold Time and frosen Fate
   Thaw us a warme seate to our rest.
VII
Our sacred harthes shall burne eternally   25
   As Vestall Flames, the North-wind, he
Shall strike his frost-stretch'd Winges, dissolve and flye
   This *Ætna* in Epitome.
VIII
Dropping *December* shall come weeping in,
   Bewayle th'usurping of his Raigne;   30
But when in show'rs of old Greeke we beginne,
   Shall crie, he hath his Crowne againe!
IX
Night as cleare *Hesper* shall our Tapers whip
   From the light Casements where we play,
And the darke Hagge from her black mantle strip,   35
   And sticke there everlasting Day.
X
Thus richer then untempted Kings are we,
   That asking nothing, nothing need:
Though Lord of all what Seas imbrace; yet he
   That wants himselfe, is poore indeed.   40

The poem is addressed by the poet "To my noble friend, Mr. Charles Cotton." It would be interesting to know more than we do about Lovelace's noble friend. The scholars do not agree as to his identity. C. H. Wilkinson thinks it was Charles Cotton, the son; C. H. Hartmann, Charles Cotton, the father. But even if we do not know the identity of the noble friend, we still can enjoy the poem and understand it.

There are, I grant, poems that do depend for their basic meaning upon some knowledge of the historical characters mentioned in them. Marvell's "Horatian Ode upon Cromwell's Return from Ireland" would be hopelessly obscure to a reader who knew absolutely nothing about Oliver Cromwell. Yet we can and must make a distinction between a poem as a personal document and as a poetic structure. For example, it is conceivable, though highly improbable, that some day a scholar may come upon a set of seventeenth-century letters that would tell us that Mr. Charles Cotton had performed several great services for our poet, and that this little poem had been written by Lovelace in grave apprehension as he received news that his friend had been stricken with a serious illness. While we are using our imaginations, let us suppose further that the letters showed that this poem was written in the hope of cheering his friend by suggesting that they had many more years of fine companionship before them. Such letters might very well enhance for us the meaning of the poem as a personal document of Lovelace's life. But if we may thus enhance a poem at will by importing into it all sorts of associations and meaning, then we can theoretically turn an obscure poem into a clear poem—and a poor poem into a good poem. As has been remarked earlier in this book, even the verse from the newspaper agony column beginning "It is now a year and day / Since little Willie went away" might move us deeply if we actually knew little Willie and his sorrowing mother. But only the unwary would take the triggering of such an emotional response as proof of the value of the poem. In the hypothetical case just cited, the response comes from the poem not as poem but as personal document. What references and allusions are legitimate parts of a poem and what are merely adventitious associations? The distinction is not always obvious, and I do not care to try to fix here a doctrinaire limitation. But I think that we shall have to agree that some limits must exist.

The first part of Lovelace's poem derives from the Anacreontic poem "The Grasshopper." (I quote the beginning lines of Cowley's translation.)

> Happy *Insect,* what can be
> In happiness compar'd to Thee?
> Fed with nourishment divine,
> The dewy *Mornings* gentle *Wine!*
> *Nature* waits upon thee still,
> And thy verdant Cup does fill,
> 'Tis fill'd where ever thou does tread,
> *Nature* selfe's *thy Ganimed.*
> Thou dost drink, and dance, and sing;
> Happier than the happiest *King!* . . .

Lovelace evidently began his poem as a free translation of the Greek poem; but he went on to develop out of it a thoroughly different poem—different in theme and different in tone. The little Anacreontic poem becomes merely a starting point for the poem Lovelace actually writes. Whereas the Greek poet contents himself with giving a charming account of the grasshopper's life, Lovelace uses the account of the grasshopper's life to set up the contrast between the spurious summer of nature and the genuine summer to which men have access. If we are interested in the way in which the poem was composed, we shall certainly want to know what sources Lovelace used, and there may be a special delight in seeing how he has reshaped his sources to his own purpose. But a mere roundup of the sources will never in itself tell us what the poet has done with them. A bad poem may assimilate Anacreon as well as a good poem. The value of a poem as a work of art is not to be determined by an account of its sources.

In the same way, the history of ideas might tell us a great deal about this poem. The historian can trace the development of such concepts as that of the actual considered to be a dim and limited reflection of the ideal—specifically, the summer of the grasshopper in the natural world of the seasons viewed as a mere shadow of the genuine summer which transcends the seasonal world of nature. The historians of ideas can trace for us the development of the concept of richness based not upon the possession of goods but upon one's freedom from wants—that is, the notion of richness as completeness. The ideas that Lovelace is using here are familiar to most readers and can be taken for granted; but I concede that the reader who is not familiar with these concepts might have serious trouble with the poem. Even so, criticism has to be distinguished from the scholarship of the history of ideas, for the obvious reason that the historian of ideas may find just as much to explain in a poor and unsuccessful poem as in a good one.

It is the critic of moralistic bias, as we have already noted, who is most likely to object sharply to modern critical procedure. The serious moralist finds it hard not to become impatient with a critic who seems to ignore the moral problems and concern himself merely with "form and technique." Nor will he necessarily be satisfied with the critic's concession that wisdom is certainly to be found in poetry. Lovelace's poem, for example, says, among other things, that happiness is not dependent upon external circumstances but is an inward quality. But the moralist argues that this is surely the doctrine that ought to be emphasized in any critical account of the poem. For it may appear to him that it is this moral truth that gives the poem its value.

But the sternest moralist will have to concede that many poems that may contain admirable doctrine—Longfellow's "Psalm of Life," for example—are very poor poems. Furthermore, if one tries to save the case by stipulating that the doctrine must not only be true, but must be rendered clearly, acceptably, and persuasively, he will come perilously close to reducing the poet's art to that of the mere rhetorician.

Moralists as diverse as the Marxists and the later nationalistic Van

Wyck Brooks are all for making the Muse a rewrite girl. But the Muse is willful and stubborn: a thesis presented eloquently and persuasively is not necessarily the same thing as a poem. "The Grasshopper" is, among other things, a document in the personal history of Lovelace, testifying to his relations with Charles Cotton. It is an instance of Lovelace's regard for the classics; it incorporates an amalgam of ideas inherited from the Christian-classical tradition of Western thought; it is an admonition to find happiness within oneself. The point is that it could be all of these things and not be a poem at all. It could be, for example, a letter from Lovelace to Charles Cotton, or an entry in Lovelace's commonplace book.

It happens to be a poem and a rather fine one. But defense of this judgment, if it were questioned, would involve an examination of the structure of the poem as poem. And with this kind of examination the so-called new criticism is concerned. I should be happy to drop the adjective *new* and simply say: with this kind of judgment, literary criticism is concerned.

Lovelace's poem is a little masterpiece in the management of tone. Lovelace makes the life of the insect thoroughly Lucullan. The grasshopper is "drunk ev'ry night": Lovelace provides him with a carved bed in which to sleep off his debauch. But actually the grasshopper is up with the dawn, for his tipple is a natural distillation, the free gift of heaven. The joys to which he abandons himself are all innocent and natural, and his merrymaking makes men merry too.

The grasshopper's life, then, though described in terms that hint at the human world, is not used to symbolize a type of human experience to be avoided. We have here no fable of the ant and the grasshopper. Lovelace would not reform the little wastrel, but delights in him, so joyously and thoughtlessly at home in his world.

Stanzas 5 and 6 define very delicately and precisely this attitude, one of humor and amusement, touched with the merest trace of pity. The grasshopper is happy because he cannot possibly foresee the harvest or the biting blasts of winter. "But ah the Sickle! Golden Eares are Cropt." Everything in the line conspires to place the emphasis upon the word *golden,* a word rich in every sort of association: wealth, ripeness, luxury, the Saturnian age of gold. But the full force of *golden* is perhaps not realized until we come to line 17: "Poore verdant foole! and now green Ice!" The clash of gold and green absorbs and carries within it the whole plight of the grasshopper. Green suggests not only the little insect's color but all that is growing, immature, unripe, and innocently simple. The

oaten ears on which the grasshopper loves to swing change, by natural
process, from green to gold; the grasshopper cannot change with them.
The mature oaten ears may resemble the precious metal—one remembers Milton's "vegetable gold"—but greenness turned to something
hard and stiff and cold—the sliver of green ice—is a pathetic absurdity.

I should not press this contrast so hard had Lovelace not insisted on
the color and emphasized its connection with springing verdure by his
phrase "Poor verdant foole!" And here it becomes proper to acknowl-
edge the critic's debt to the lexicographer and to concede that my suggestion that *verdant* means *gullible* has no specific dictionary warrant.
The Oxford Dictionary's first entry for this sense of *verdant* is as late as
1824; the same distinct dictionary, however, does indicate that *green*
could carry these connotations as early as 1548. In the context of this
poem, *verdant,* followed by the phrase "green ice," and associated as it is
with "foole," must surely carry the meaning of inexperienced, thoughtless innocence.

The gentle and amused irony that suffuses "Poor verdant foole" continues through the lines that follow: The grasshopper's joys are measured by the instability of the insects' precarious perch—"Large and as
lasting, as thy Peirch of Grasse." But the speaker soon turns from his
contemplation of these ephemeral joys to man's perdurable joys—from
the specious summer of nature to the genuine summer that he and his
noble friend can create, each in the other's breast.

The poem pivots sharply in the fifth stanza, and the management of
tone is so dexterous that we may be tempted to pass over the last half of
the poem too easily. But these latter stanzas have their difficulties, and if
we want to understand the poem I think we shall want to find precisely
what goes on. Moreover, these stanzas present their problem of tone
also. The poem must not seem smug and sanctimonious; man's happiness must not seem too easily achieved. For if man rises superior to the
animal kingdom, he is not, for all of that, a disembodied spirit. He is
animal, too, and he has to reckon with the "frost-stretch'd Winges" of
the North Wind and with the blackness of the winter night. Moreover,
as man, he has his peculiar bugbears of a sort that the grasshopper does
not have to contend with. There is at least a hint of this in the reference
to "untempted Kings."

As a general comment, suffice it to say that in this poem the flesh is
given its due: the warm hearth, the lighted casements, and showers of
"old Greeke" fortify the friends against the winter night and give a sense
of real gaiety and mirth. If there is high thinking, the living is not so

plain as to be unconvincing. And the sentiment on which the poem closes is none the less serious because it comes out of festivity and has been warmed by wine. He who "wants himselfe" is poor indeed. It is this full possession of himself, this lack of dependence upon things, which makes him richer than "untempted Kings."

The last phrase, however, is curious. In this context, Lovelace ought to be writing to his friend: "since we are untempted by material possessions, we are actually richer than kings." The force of the contrast depends upon the fact that kings are more than most men tempted by material possessions. Why then *untempted* kings? The solution is probably to be sought in the source of the poem. In the Anacreontic "Grasshopper" the insect is referred to as a king—the Greek text has βασιλεὺς—and Lovelace's contemporary Abraham Cowley uses the word *king* in his translation. Lovelace, then, for his fit audience who knew the Greek poem, is saying: we are like the grasshopper, that rare specimen, an untempted king; but we are richer than he, since our joys do not end with the natural summer, but last on through the genuine (and unending) summer of the heart.

But it is stanzas 8 and 9 that cause the real trouble. As C. H. Hartmann remarks: "Lovelace himself could on occasion become so involved as to be utterly incomprehensible even without the assistance of an eccentric printer."[1] To deal first with stanza 9: the drift of the argument is plain enough, but Lovelace's editor, Wilkinson, also confesses to difficulties here: the friends will whip night away from their casements. But what are we to make of the phrase "as cleare *Hesper*"? Wilkinson writes, "The meaning would seem to be that 'just as Hesperus shines clearer as the day draws to a close, so will our tapers whip night from the lighted casements of the room where we amuse ourselves.'" But I fail to see the relevance of his argument that Hesper shines the brighter as the skies darken. Why not simply read "as clear Hesper" as an ellipsis for "as clear Hesper does"? Our tapers will whip night away as clear Hesper whips it away. Moreover, the poet chooses as the dispeller of gloom the modest light of the star just because it is modest. He is not claiming that he and his friend can abolish winter. "Dropping December" *shall* come weeping in. The friendly association with Cotton will not do away with the wintry night. What the human being can do is to rid the night of its horror—exorcise the hag [the nightmare]—maintain a small circle of

1. Cyril H. Hartmann, *The Cavalier Spirit and Its Influence on the Life and Work of Richard Lovelace*, 117.

light amid the enveloping darkness. This is what the evening star, clear Hesper, does, and all that he and his friend with their gleaming tapers propose to do. As with light, so with heat. Their hearth will be Aetna, but an Aetna is "Epitome"—a tiny volcano of heat. The poet is very careful not to claim too much.

Stanza 8 contains the most difficult passage in the poem, and Lovelace's editors have not supplied a note. "Dropping *December*" means *dripping,* or *rainy,* December. But why will December lament the usurping of his reign? Does the warm fire and pleasant company maintained by the two friends constitute the usurpation against which he will protest? We may at first be inclined to think so, but the lines that follow make it plain that December is not crying out against, but rejoicing in, the two friends' festivities. Seeing them at their wine, December exclaims that he has "his Crowne againe." But what is December's crown? One looks for it throughout Greek and Roman mythology in vain.

We have here, I am convinced, a topical allusion. The crown of December is evidently the Christmas festivities, festivities actually more ancient than Christianity—the age-old feast of the winter solstice of which the Roman Saturnalia is an instance. December's crown is indeed a venerable one. And who has stolen December's crown—who usurped his reign? The Puritans, by abolishing the celebration of Christmas. We remember that it is a Cavalier poet writing, and I suspect, if we care to venture at dating the poem, we shall have to put it at some time between the Puritan abolition of Christmas in 1642 and the publication of Lovelace's *Lucasta* in 1649. Line 23, then, "And spite of this cold Time and frosen Fate," is seen to refer to more than the mere winter season. It must allude to the Puritan domination—for Lovelace, a cold time and frozen fate indeed. I would not press the historical allusion. The poem is certainly not primarily an anti-Puritan poem. The basic contrast is made between animal life and the higher and more enduring joys to which man can attain. But a casual allusion to the troubled state of England would be a thoroughly natural one for the poet of "To Althea from Prison" to have written, and nowhere more appropriately than here, in a poem to a close friend.

The reader may not be convinced by this interpretation of the eighth stanza. Very frankly, my basic concern has been to read the poem, not to seek out historical allusions. But an honest concern with the text characterizes, or ought to characterize, the work of both scholar and critic. In view of the much-advertised quarrel between scholarship and criticism, the point is worth stressing. The critic selects from scholarship those things that will help him understand the poem qua poem; in some matters the contribution of the scholar may be indispensable. Literary criticism and literary scholarship are therefore natural allies in their concern to understand the poem; they may at points coalesce. But if, because of unavoidable specialization, the scholar and critic cannot always be one and the same man, I think it a pity if, with shortsighted jealousy, they elbow each other as rivals and combatants.

Earlier I said that recent criticism had attempted to focus attention on the poem rather than upon the poet or upon the reader. But there is no danger that people will cease to talk about the poet and his reader. Our basic human interest is most readily served when we talk about the reader's reactions, about our own responses to the poem or the novel—the chill down our spine, or perhaps the special sensation in the pit of the stomach that A. E. Housman claimed to experience when he encountered a genuine poem. Human interest may be almost as readily served if we talk about the personality of the author. Such talk may include everything from Lord Byron's amours to the possible effects of Keats's tuberculosis upon his personality—everything from Shakespeare's alleged Oedipus complex to Robert Frost's love for New Hampshire.

No one wants to forbid either the study of the author or the study of the reader. Both kinds of study are legitimate and have their own interest. In view of the present state of criticism, it may be somewhat more to the point to say a final word in justification of recent stress upon the poem as such.

A study of the reader's reactions may be most interesting and illuminating. But concentration on the reader's reactions tends to take us away from the work of art into the domain of reader psychology. We ask why Keats's "Ode on a Grecian Urn" provokes the different responses that it does, and we find the answer in the differing psychological makeup of the various readers. Or we may ask why certain aspects of Shakespeare were praised in the eighteenth century and others in the nineteenth, and typically find our answer in the differing cultural climates of the two centuries. But even though a poem may be realized only through some reader's response to it, the proper study of the poem is the study of the poem.

A study of the poet's personality and intellectual background will almost certainly be rewarding. After all, the poem is an expression of the mind and sensibility of the man who writes it, and may well reflect his cultural background and the spirit of his age. Yet concentration upon these matters can also take us away from the poem—into author psychology or the history of ideas or cultural history. In any case, it is valuable to ponder the fact that we often know very little about the author's experience beyond what he has been able to catch and make permanent within the poem. We know, for example, very little about Richard Lovelace. About the greatest of our poets, Shakespeare, we know even less—if we exclude what we may surmise from the works themselves. Even where we know a great deal about the author's personality and ideas, *we rarely know as much as the poem itself can tell us about itself;* for the poem is no mere effusion of a personality. It is a construct—an articulation of ideas and emotions—a dramatization. It is not a slice of raw experience but a product of the poet's imagination—not merely something suffered by him but the result of his creative activity. As a work of art, it calls for a reciprocal imaginative activity on our part; and that involves seeing it for what it *is.*

Postscript (1990)

The foregoing essay was delivered on 23 April 1959 as a lecture to a special seminar arranged by the poet Stanley Burnshaw. It was not published, however, until 1962, in a volume Burnshaw edited entitled *Varieties of Literary Criticism.*

When I was writing my account of the Lovelace poem, I was not aware that the late Don Cameron Allen, of Johns Hopkins University, had, two years before, published an article entitled "An Explication of Lovelace's 'The Grassehopper.'"

What I want to call attention to here is that a distinguished literary historian and a literary critic reputed to be careless of, and even hostile to, the biographical and historical background of a poem could, quite independently, come to the same solution of the problem of December's "Crowne."

On reflection, however, it ought not seem at all strange that this should be so. Any serious attempt to get at the meaning of individual words or phrases or images might be expected to yield much the same meanings, whether the scholar was primarily concerned with the historical background or the critic with the unity and wholeness of a poem and its literary worth. The truth is that these concerns are rarely completely diverse. Professor Allen was obviously very much interested in the literary qualities of "The Grasse-Hopper," and I certainly was not devoid of interest in the cultural matrix out of which the poem came.

To help the reader make a more just comparison of the two accounts of the poem, I have reprinted, with only a few very minor revisions, my 1962 discussion of "The Grasse-Hopper." The reader interested in making a detailed comparison of my account and Allen's should be told that Allen's essay is also available in *Seventeenth Century English Poetry,* edited by W. R. Keast. In many respects the two essays do differ, and some of the differences represent differences of approach. In what follows, I shall comment upon a few of them.

Allen associates December's crown with the crown worn by the "Prince Christmas," who was annually chosen to preside over the Christmas festivities. He cites a very interesting account of these festivities as they were observed in Oxford University in 1607. Since Lovelace had been a student at Oxford, Allen suggests that Lovelace may well be remembering the Oxford festivities at Christmastime. I note that Anthony à Wood, Oxford's seventeenth-century historian, also, according to J. E. V. Crofts's "A Life of Bishop Corbett," gives an account of the election of Christmas "Princes" at the Oxford colleges.

Lovelace must have known of Oxford's Christmas Princes. In his poem, however, Lovelace does not speak of the crown of the Christmas Prince but of December's crown. The personified month rejoices that he has regained the crown that the Puritans had despoiled him of in doing away with the celebration of Christmas. In short, in the poem the reference to the crown is not at all to the crown worn by the Christmas Prince, but to the great feast that crowned the month of December, whether it bore a Christian or a pagan meaning.

The reference to a crown of which the wearer had been despoiled causes Allen to think not only of the Puritans who had removed December's "Crowne," but of King Charles, from whom the Puritan party had removed not only his crown but also his head. Allen goes on to say that Lovelace's poem is "not a poem about a grasshopper but about a king and a cause that are dead on earth but living in Heaven." The Greek poet had called the grasshopper a king, but Allen associates the insect with a specific king, Charles Stuart. In what follows, we shall see how he accomplishes this feat.

In the course of his essay, Allen provides us—with truly remarkable learning—with what would appear to be an exhaustive collection of the references made by the classical authors to the grasshopper. Among others, Allen cites Homer, Plato, Thucydides, Diogenes, Lucretius, Theocritus, and a number of the poets represented in the *Greek Anthology*. From a consideration of such authorities, Allen summarizes the characteristics of the grasshopper as they were viewed in antiquity. The grasshopper was, he says, "a singer beloved of the muses," a creature that had once been a human artist, a "badge of royalty, an aristocrat, and a poet." Moreover, Allen points out that in Greek literature this insect "had an easy connection with men in disfavor."

This sheaf of classical associations induces Allen to believe that Lovelace, writing his poem at a time when the Royalist cause had collapsed, associated the grasshopper with the doomed Charles I. This conclusion, however, surely claims too much. If we take into account all the various things that the grasshopper meant to the poets of antiquity, we are more than embarrassed with riches: we are fairly suffocated. Granted that a classically educated Englishman of the seventeenth century conceivably had at his disposal so many varied conceptions on which to draw, one feels compelled to ask which of these are pertinent to the poem? For example, with reference to identifying Charles I with the grasshopper, should we not keep closer both to the Anacreontic poem and to the facts of history?

Could, for example, Lovelace possibly have addressed his king as "Poore verdant foole"? Lovelace is no Andrew Marvell, but even Marvell, whose attitude toward Charles was sufficiently detached and complicated, never approached anything like such a degree of pitying dismissal. Mr. Geoffrey Grigson, a cantankerous Englishman of our own day who is given to speaking his mind, has recently come close to calling Charles "a fool." He describes him as "a vacillating, mincing aesthete, who had a good eye for pictures." But such an outburst does not help Allen's case, nor would Allen himself have been willing to accept it as supporting evidence.

"Poore verdant foole" in the context in which it appears in Lovelace's poem might be thought to hint at the fable of the prudent, hardworking ant and the wastrel grasshopper, and Allen provides a detailed note tracing the fable back as far as Seneca. But Allen is surely right in refusing to interpret Lovelace's poem as stressing the moral of the fable. Nevertheless, "Poor verdant foole" does sharply undercut the concept of the grasshopper as a creature who is an aristocrat and a king.

Consider the sense in which the grasshopper is said to be a king. The Anacreontic poem indicates why he deserves to be reckoned as such. Here are the relevant lines:

βασιλεὺς, ὅπως, ἀείσεις
Ἐὰ γὰρ ἐστὶ κεῖνα πάντα
ὁἦόσα βλέπεις ἐν χγροῖς
χ' ὁπόσα φερῶσιν ὦραι.

An awkward but quite literal translation into English might read: "You sing as if a king, for all those things are yours, as many as you look upon in the fields and as many as the seasons bring." In short, the grasshopper sings like a king because he is the monarch of all that he surveys. "Uneasy lies the head that wears a crown." But not his. He sleeps soundly every night. All his needs are freely supplied to him by nature. There is nothing that he could wish for that is not his for the taking. The Greek poem, though full of other commendations of the insect's blessed estate, makes no further reference to him as a king.

Moreover, if one examines Lovelace's adaptation of the Greek poem, he will see that Lovelace never actually addresses the grasshopper as a king. It is only by implication that he ever makes him out to be king, and then not until the last stanza of the poem. When the poet writes that he and his friend are richer than "untempted Kings," he does imply that the grasshopper is a king—in fact, that the grasshopper is that rarity, an untempted king. How, then, are the two friends sitting by their cheerful fire happier than this untempted king? Because they are not, like the grasshopper, at the mercy of wintry nature, but possess a resource not available to other creatures.

The three lines with which the poem closes make this last point explicitly. Though the two friends do resemble the grasshopper in needing nothing and asking for nothing, their happiness is not limited to the insect's one brief summer; they enjoy "A Genuine Summer," that to be found only within the heart and mind. This all-important contrast between the world of nature and the inner world of mind and spirit attainable by the human being receives a final stress in the last two lines: the truly rich man is not the man who owns a whole world of things, but the one who exercises a lordship over himself. In short, Lovelace's treatment of the royal estate of the grasshopper is selective, indirect, and pointedly specific.

It is worth noting how radically different is Lovelace's poem from that of his contemporary Abraham Cowley. Whereas Lovelace emphasizes the difference between the genuine summer possible to mankind and the brief summer of nature—all that is given to the insect to enjoy—Cowley makes a virtue of the fact that his grasshopper will die with the coming of winter:

> To thee of all things upon earth,
> *Life* is no longer than thy *Mirth*.
> Happy *Insect,* happy Thou,
> Dost neither *Age,* nor *Winter* know.

Cowley calls the grasshopper an "Epicurean Animal," who, when "Sated with thy *Summer Feast, /* . . . retir'est to endless *Rest.*"[2]

A good concise account of the philosophical ideas involved in Lovelace's "The Grasse-hopper" is to be found in a book that appeared some years after the publication of Allen's essay and of mine. Isabel Rivers, in her *Classical and Christian Ideas in English Renaissance Poetry,* cites "The Grass-hopper" as an expression of Stoicism. She writes that the English poet of the period "most influenced by Stoic Ethics" was Ben Jonson, and that he "preferred Seneca among Stoic authors. . . . His Stoic poems assume that there is a small circle of good men who hold themselves aloof from their society and stand firm in the face of changeable fortune. . . . There is a more restricted use of Stoic attitudes and vocabulary in Cavalier poets like Lovelace . . . , forced into retirement by the Civil War. However, the Stoicism of the Cavaliers is diluted with Epicureanism, and owes more to Horace than to Seneca."[2]

* * *

I have indicated earlier why I have chosen to reprint my 1962 discussion of the poem in its original form. But it may not be amiss to set down some of the additions and corrections that, writing it today, I would want to make. A number of problematic lines and passages demand that a commentator should at least make an attempt to deal with them. What, for example, is the significance of "to thy Carv'd Acron-bed to lye" (line 8)? Lovelace obviously means to provide his grasshopper with a comfortably appropriate bed. But what is an "Acron" bed? *Acron* is a well-attested variant of *acorn;* yet is Lovelace suggesting that grasshoppers sleep in acorn shells, or rather the delicately modeled little cap that crowns an acorn? I wonder whether even the smallest grasshopper (or

---

2. Isabel Rivers, *Classical and Christian Ideas in English Renaissance Poetry,* 49.

cicada, if that is what the Greek poet meant) could get inside a receptacle so small.

There are a number of other words that may puzzle a modern reader. For most of these the *OED* provides sufficient help. Thus, the "guiltplats" of the sun's beams in which the grasshopper sports are "flat ornament[s] of gold or other precious metal." The word "strike" in stanza 7, according to the *OED* (17), means to "lower or take down (a sail, mast, yard, etc.)." As used in the poem, "strike" may carry a hint of the further meaning given by the *OED:* "to lower (the topsail) . . . as a sign of surrender in [a naval] engagement."

Like so many poems of this period, the finer points of Lovelace's poem have been obscured through so many of his words having shifted their meanings. When these earlier meanings are restored, passages that seem turgid and strained become clear and natural. Even the crabbedness of the grammar about which Hartmann complains is often cleared up. Thus, "dissolve" in stanza 7 is here used in its intransitive sense: "to vanish or disappear gradually, come to an end" (*OED* 13).

The "show'rs of old Greeke" (stanza 8) are also a problem. Wilkinson takes the "old Greeke" to be Greek wine of a proper vintage, and in my 1962 essay I followed him. (Allen would seem to hold the same view, though his comments on the point are somewhat ambiguous.) In later years I have come to have my doubts about this interpretation. The difficulty is twofold: I can't believe that at this period Greek wine was often, or perhaps ever, imported into England. It seems quite improbable. Crofts, in his "Life of Bishop Corbett," writes that the young wits and gentlemen of the time at Oxford scorned the alehouse as the haunt of low company and at a tavern drank canary wine.

In the second place, *Greek* used as a substantive seems invariably to refer to the language. It may be that the word *showers* ("Show'rs of old Greeke") has influenced readers to assume that the "Old Greeke" must be a liquid of some kind. But in Lovelace's day *shower* could mean simply "a copious or liberal supply bestowed" (*OED* 3). In sum, I suggest that the "o'reflowing glasse" mentioned in stanza 5 brimmed over with a wine such as sack or canary, say, and that the "show'rs of old Greeke" were not potations at all but quotations from Anacreon and the other ancient Greek poets and philosophers.

Perhaps a more difficult problem in stanza 8 is the meaning of "beginne." What is it that the two friends begin to do? The *OED* again provides help. An early meaning of the verb was "to begin a speech, to start speaking, to speak." Thus, it seems more plausible to assume that the two friends begin to speak in Greek or at least to quote from classical Greek poetry, rather than to assume that they begin to drink Greek wine.

The "Grasse-Hopper" is a beautifully controlled poem. The handling of tone is delicate but firm. Indeed, I think that it is one of its author's best poems. It indicates a scope of reflection and philosophical maturity beyond what most of us think of as Lovelace's domain. It needs, and very properly engages, the full energies of both the cultural historian and the literary critic as well as those of the reader who simply wants to enjoy a charming poem.

IX

Poetry and History

Andrew Marvell

An *Horatian* Ode upon *Cromwel's* Return from *Ireland*

> The forward Youth that would appear
> Must now forsake his *Muses* dear,
>   Nor in the Shadows sing
>   His Numbers languishing.
> 'Tis time to leave the Books in dust,   5
> And oyl th' unused Armours rust:
>   Removing from the Wall
>   The Corslet of the Hall.
> So restless *Cromwel* could not cease
> In the inglorious Arts of Peace,   10
>   But through adventrous War
>   Urged his active Star:
> And, like the three-fork'd Lightning, first
> Breaking the Clouds where it was nurst,
>   Did thorough his own Side   15
>   His fiery way divide.
> For 'tis all one to Courage high
> The Emulous or Enemy;
>   And with such to inclose
>   Is more then to oppose.   20
> Then burning through the Air he went,
> And Pallaces and Temples rent:
>   And *Cæsars* head at last
>   Did through his Laurels blast.
> 'Tis Madness to resist or blame   25
> The force of angry Heavens flame;
>   And, if we would speak true,
>   Much to the Man is due:
> Who, from his private Gardens, where

He liv'd reserved and austere,   30
   As if his hightest plot
   To plant the Bergamot,
Could by industrious Valour climbe
To ruine the great Work of Time,
   And cast the Kingdoms old   35
   Into another Mold.
Though Justice against Fate complain,
And plead the antient Rights in vain:
   But those do hold or break
   As Men are strong or weak.   40
Nature that hateth emptiness,
Allows of penetration less:
   And therefore must make room
   Where greater Spirits come.
What Field of all the Civil Wars   45
Where his were not the deepest Scars?
   And *Hampton* shows what part
   He had of wiser Art:
Where, twining subtile fears with hope,
He wove a Net of such a scope,   50
   That *Charles* himself might chase
   To *Caresbrooks* narrow case:
That thence the *Royal Actor* born
The *Tragick Scaffold* might adorn,
   While round the armed Bands   55
   Did clap their bloody hands.
He nothing common did, or mean,
Upon the memorable Scene:
   But with his keener Eye
   The Axes edge did try: 60
Nor call'd the *Gods* with vulgar spight
To vindicate his helpless Right,
   But bow'd his comely Head
   Down, as upon a Bed.
This was that memorable Hour   65
Which first assur'd the forced Pow'r.
   So when they did design
   The *Capitols* first Line,
A bleeding Head where they begun,
Did fright the Architects to run;   70
   And yet in that the *State*
   Foresaw its happy Fate.

And now the *Irish* are asham'd
To see themselves in one Year tam'd:
    So much one Man can do,   75
    That does both act and know.
They can affirm his Praises best,
And have, though overcome, confest
    How good he is, how just,
    And fit for highest Trust: 80
Nor yet grown stiffer with Command,
But still in the *Republick's* hand:
    How fit he is to sway
    That can so well obey.
He to the *Commons Feet* presents   85
A *Kingdome,* for his first years rents:
    And, what he may, forbears
    His Fame to make it theirs:
And has his Sword and Spoyls ungirt,
To lay them at the *Publick's* skirt.   90
    So when the Falcon high
    Falls heavy from the Sky,
She, having kill'd, no more does search,
But on the next green Bow to pearch;
    Where, when he first does lure,   95
    The Falckner has her sure.
What may not then our *Isle* presume
While Victory his Crest does plume;
    What may not others fear,
    If thus he crown each Year!   100
A *Cæsar* he ere long to *Gaul,*
To *Italy,* an *Hannibal,*
    And to all States not free
    Shall *Clymacterick* be.
The *Pict* no shelter now shall find   105
Within his party-colour'd Mind;
    But from this Valour sad
    Shrink underneath the Plad:
Happy if in the tufted brake
The *English Hunter* him mistake,   110
    Nor lay his Hounds in near
    The *Caledonian* Deer.
But thou the Wars and Fortunes Son
March indefatigably on,
    And for the last effect   115

Still keep thy Sword erect:
Besides the force it has to fright
The Spirits of the shady Night;
The same *Arts* that did *gain*
A *Pow'r* must it *maintain*.   120

This great poem makes a fitting choice with which to conclude an examination of poems that claim the attention of the historian as well as of the literary critic. The "Ode" is obviously saturated in the history of the times, and a proper historical knowledge is absolutely necessary if we are to understand it. Yet such knowledge alone will not of itself unlock for us the totality of the poem—or even its true meaning. A reader, drawing on his knowledge of Cromwell, Charles, and Andrew Marvell, can impose upon the "Ode" things that are demonstrably not there. In any case, essential though it be, knowledge of the historical background as such cannot, for example, explain why the "Ode" is so much finer a poem than Marvell's "On the First Anniversary of the Government under His Highness the Lord Protector, 1655."

For our purposes the "Ode" is also a good choice because its title enables us to date it rather precisely. Cromwell's victorious Irish campaign had required only nine months, and Cromwell was now back in England in May of 1650. Not long after his return, trouble erupted in Scotland, and Cromwell invaded Scotland on July 22. Since his success over the Scots could scarcely have been assumed before his victory won at Dunbar on September 3, the "Ode" must have been written some time between late May and late August of 1650.

The "Ode" also makes a strong demand on the literary critic, for he must deal with the tone of the poem, and therefore with the speaker's attitude toward both Charles and Cromwell. The attitudes of human beings, of course, are subject to change, and we must not incautiously assume that Andrew Marvell's attitude toward Cromwell in the summer of 1650 was what one presumes it was in, say, 1655, when he wrote the "First Anniversary." Nor, of course, can we assume that his attitude was necessarily the same as in the 1640s, when most of Marvell's associates appear to have been Royalists. There seems general agreement that during this period his own sympathies were Royalist, and apparently they continued to be so down through 1649. For example, he contributed a laudatory poem to the publication of *Lucasta,* a collection of poems by that ardent Cavalier poet Sir Richard Lovelace, and in the same year he was associated with a number of Royalist poets in publishing verse tributes to Lord Hastings, another Royalist, who had died in 1649.

If we add to these poems the "Elegy upon the Death of My Lord

Francis Villiers," a Cavalier who had been killed fighting for the king in 1649, the Royalist bias becomes quite explicit. As H. M. Margoliouth puts it: "If [the "Elegy on Villiers"] is Marvell's, it is his one unequivocal royalist utterance; it throws into strong relief the transitional character of *An Horatian Ode* where royalist principles and admiration for Cromwell the Great Man exist side by side."[1] (Of Marvell's most recent editors, Professor Elizabeth Donno regards the poem as Marvell's; Professor George de F. Lord places it among those of doubtful authorship.)

Christopher Hill, in his excellent essay "Society and Andrew Marvell" (1946), agrees that when Marvell returned to England from his travels on the Continent, which would be about 1646–1647, his sympathies "were apparently Royalist. But [he adds] we have no real evidence for his activities, and little for his views, until 1650, the year after the execution of Charles I"—which brings us up to the "Horatian Ode" itself.

Before getting into that and, in the course of it, taking up Hill's own view of the poem, I might mention two other bits of evidence that Hill could not take into account. In a 1946 lecture (published in 1947) I pointed out that Robert Wild, in his poem "The Death of Mr. Christopher Love," echoed two memorable lines from the "Horatian Ode." Love was beheaded at Cromwell's orders on August 22, 1651, and one assumes that the poem was written shortly after his execution.

Marvell's couplet "But with his keener Eye / The Axes edge did try" becomes in Wild's poem: "His keener Words did their sharp Ax exceed." Since the "Horatian Ode" did not achieve print until 1681, Wild must have seen a manuscript copy, which means that such copies were being handed about in Royalist circles, for Wild was a Presbyterian Royalist.

In my 1947 version of that essay I also noted that Marvell probably derived the special stanza of his "Ode" from Sir Richard Fanshawe, who was, as we have noted earlier, a devoted Royalist. Marvell used this stanza only in the "Ode," and Margoliouth had thought it likely that it was Marvell's own invention. Just possibly it was. But Fanshawe, in his *Selected Parts of Horace . . . Now newly put into English,* 1652, uses the stanza a number of times—which might suggest that Fanshawe borrowed it from Marvell. But in 1952 William Simeone reported that "An Oade. Splendidis longum valedico nugis," found among Fanshawe's papers and almost certainly written by him some time between 1626 and 1631, uses this stanza form.[2] Whichever was the borrower, a Royalist connection is suggested; and furthermore, if

1. H. M. Margoliouth, ed., *The Poems and Letters of Andrew Marvell,* 1:334.
2. "A Probable Antecedent of Marvell's Horatian Ode."

the borrower was Marvell, he had to have seen Fanshawe's employment of the stanza in manuscript copies. So much for the evidence of Marvell's Royalist sympathies in the summer of 1650 prior to the "Horatian Ode."

One more piece of such evidence remains to be dealt with, though this one is to be found in a poem written some months after the composition of the "Ode." It is Marvell's poem entitled "Tom May's Death." Thomas May, the dramatist and translator, died on November 13, 1650. George Lord, presumably because the poem does not appear in the Popple manuscript, in his edition places it among the "Poems of Doubtful Authorship." But Elizabeth Donno regards it as Marvell's, and William Wallace and Christopher Hill, in their important discussions of the "Horatian Ode," also assume that it is his.

The point of this witty and bitter satire is that May was a turncoat and a time-serving poet. He had earlier sought royal favor and had dedicated three works to King Charles; but in the 1640s, having failed to be named poet laureate, he had become a defender of the Parliamentary party and had published a *History of the Parliament* and *A Breviary of the History of the Parliament.*

If "Tom May's Death" was not written by Marvell himself, it is odd that the unknown author has apparently copied a number of phrasings right out of the "Horatian Ode." Lines 63–76 will furnish striking examples.

> When the Sword glitters ore the Judges head,
> And fear has Coward Churchman silenced,
> Then is the Poets time, 'tis then he drawes,
> And single fights forsaken vertues cause.
> He, when the wheel of Empire whirleth back,
> And though the World's disjointed Axel crack,
> Sings still of ancient Rights and better Times,
> Seeks wretched good, arraigns successful Crimes.
> But thou base man first prostituted hast
> Our spotless knowledge and the studies chaste,
> Apostatizing from our Arts and us,
> To turn the Chronicler to *Spartacus.*
> Yet wast thou taken hence with equal fate,
> Before thou couldst great Charles his death relate.

The last couplet requires a brief note. In his *Breviary of the History of the Parliament* May breaks off his narration just before an account of the execution of Charles I. Now that sudden death has taken off May himself, he will never be able to complete that narration—which the satiric poet implies is a mercy. We, his readers, will at least be spared that.

These lines might well have come from a Royalist's pen, and most probably did come from that of Marvell, who in the "Ode" had paid a fitting tribute to Charles's noble conduct on the scaffold and had dared to sing of "antient Rights" that were pleaded in vain in the face of a "forced Pow'r" and of Charles's "helpless Right" as Cromwell accomplished the "ruine [of] the great Work of Time."

Marvell's relation to May goes deeper still. Marvell had evidently read May's translation of Lucan with interest and care. Convincing proof is to be found in notes printed by Margoliouth. He there quotes from two correspondents to the *Times Literary Supplement.* I quote from the first part of this note.

> Marvell perhaps had in mind both the Latin . . . and Tom May's translation [of Lucan's *Pharsalia,* 1.144 and following], which here reads as follows (2nd edition, 1631):
>
> > But restlesse valour, and in warre a shame
> > Not to be Conquerour; fierce, not curb'd at all,
> > Ready to fight, where hope, or anger call,
> > His forward Sword; confident of successe,
> > And bold the favour of the gods to presse:
> > Orethrowing all that his ambition stay,
> > And loves that ruine should enforce his way;
> > As lightning by the winde forc'd from a cloude
> > Breakes through the wounded aire with thunder loud,
> > Disturbes the Day, the people terrifyes,
> > And by a light oblique dazels our eyes,
> > Not *Joves owne* Temple spares it; when no force,
> > No barre can hinder his prevailing course,
> > Great waste, as foorth it sallyes and retires,
> > It makes and gathers his dispersed fires.
>
> Note the verbal resemblances, "restless valour," and "industrious Valour," "forward Sword" and "The forward Youth," "lightning . . . from a cloude Breakes" and "lightning . . . Breaking the Clouds."[3]

The verbal resemblances are striking, but the conceptual likeness

3. Margoliouth, ed., *Poems and Letters,* 1:237–38.

between Lucan's Caesar and Marvell's Cromwell is also striking. In the "Ode," for someone like Cromwell of "Courage high," it is "all one" whether

> The Emulous or Enemy;
> And with such to inclose
> Is more then to oppose.

Lucan's Caesar counts it

> in warre a shame
> Not to be Conquerour; fierce, not curb'd at all.

He will brook no impediment whatever. Cromwell, like the lightning, burned through the air

> And Pallaces and Temples rent:
> And Cæsars [Charles I's] head at last
> Did through his Laurels blast.

Lucan's Caesar, like the lightning, doesn't spare Jove's own Temple, since

> no force,
> No barre can hinder his prevailing course.

The general resemblances between Lucan's *Pharsalia* and the "Horatian Ode" are also strong. Both are poems about a civil war, that between Julius Caesar and Pompey and that between King and Parliament. Among other things, Marvell's evident debt to Lucan, directly and through May's translation, contributes to the prevailing Roman cast of his "Ode." The very fact that Marvell knew May's work so well may have contributed to his bitterness toward May's having turned renegade. Marvell had thought he had a right to expect better of May than this. I am inclined to believe that in the year or so that followed the execution of Charles, Marvell was obsessed with the problem of the poet's function in such troubled times, and that both of Marvell's poems of 1650, the "Ode" and "Tom May's Death," though so different in tone, are closely related and came out of the same state of mind.

Thus far I have dealt largely with the historical circumstances to which the "Ode" refers, and with some of Marvell's sources, and I have hazarded some guesses as to what Marvell the man meant to say in his poem. It is time now to turn more directly to the poem itself, and to the poetic mode of expressing matters. Thus, among other things, problems of tone and imagery come up, as does the problem of unity. These are matters that specifically call for the attention of the literary critic.

The problem of unity may be the most difficult of all. Pierre Legouis in 1928 provided an excellent and carefully measured account of the "Horatian Ode" in his *André Marvell: Poète, puritain, patriote, 1621–1678.* (I quote below from his abridged translation into English of 1965.) He tells the reader,

> This examination of a man [Cromwell], the object then and since of such conflicting judgements, has the merit of complete independence, nay, of an almost inhuman aloofness. If the poet errs in his interpretations or previsions it is not because the hero dazzles him or the regicide horrifies him. For the only time in his life he speaks *sine ira et studio,* and for over two centuries he remains the only one to have thus spoken of those events.[4]

This is an admirably succinct summary of the gist of the poem, though I think "almost inhuman aloofness" overstates the case.

I applaud, too, Legouis's refusal to see the Cromwell of the poem depicted as "a kind of Scourge of God, since there is nothing Christian in this ode"—nothing, at least, that is specifically Christian. But I believe that Legouis might have paid more attention to the detail of the poem. Some of the detail seems to me important not only for strengthening Legouis's own case but also for giving richness and body to the poem.

To turn to Margoliouth's summary, he describes the "Ode" as follows:

> The ode is the utterance of a constitutional monarchist, whose sympathies have been with the King, but who yet believes more in men than in parties or principles, and whose hopes are fixed now on Cromwell, seeing in him both the civic ideal of a ruler without personal ambition, and the man of destiny moved by and yet himself driving . . . a power which is above justice.[5]

This statement is plausible and, for its own purpose, perhaps just. But does it take us very far—even on the level of understanding Marvell the

---

4. Pierre Legouis, *André Marvell: Poète, puritain, patriote, 1621–1678*, 14–15.
5. Margoliouth, ed., *Poems and Letters*, 1:236.

man? What sort of constitutional monarchist is it who "believes more in men than in . . . principles"? Or who can accept a "power which is above justice"? I do not say that such a monarchist cannot exist. My point is that Margoliouth's statement raises more problems than it solves. Furthermore, in what sense are the speaker's hopes "fixed . . . on Cromwell"? And how confident is the speaker of the poem that Cromwell is "without personal ambition"? Margoliouth had also described the "Ode" as a poem "where royalist principles and admiration for Cromwell the Great Man exist side by side." I think that they do exist side by side, but if so, how are they related? Do they exist in separate layers, or are they somehow unified? Unified, in some sense, they must be if the "Ode" is a poem and not a heap of fragments.

From historical evidence alone one would suppose that Marvell's attitude toward Cromwell would be a rather complex one, and that this complexity would be reflected in a certain ambiguity even in the compliments paid to Cromwell. Thus, it is the "forward Youth's" attention that the voice in the poem would direct to the example of Cromwell. "Forward" may mean no more than "high-spirited," "ardent," "properly ambitious"; but the *OED* (8) sanctions the possibility that there lurks in the word the sense of "bold," even "presumptuous." The forward youth can no longer now "in the Shadows sing / His Numbers languishing." In the light of Cromwell's career, he must forsake the shadows and his "*Muses* dear" and become a man of action.

The speaker, one observes, does not identify Cromwell as the "forward Youth," or say directly that Cromwell's career has been motivated by a striving for fame. But the implications of the first two stanzas do carry over to Cromwell. There is, for example, the important word *so* in line 9 to relate Cromwell to these stanzas: "So restless Cromwel could not cease." And the darker connotations of "restless" are more prominent than those of "forward." For, though "restless" can mean simply "scorning indolence," "willing to forego ease," it can also mean "constantly stirring or acting, or desirous to be so, averse to being quiet or settled" (*OED* 2). "To cease" is used intransitively and means "to take rest, or to be or remain at rest." Cromwell's "Courage high" will not allow him to rest "in the inglorious Arts of Peace." And this implied thirst for glory is developed further in lines 33–34:

> Could by industrious Valour climbe
> To ruine the great Work of Time.

"Climbe" certainly connotes a kind of aggressiveness. In saying this we need not be afraid that we are reading into the word some smack of the modern implications. Marvell's translation of the second chorus of Seneca's *Thyestes* sufficiently attests that the word could have such associations for him:

> Climb at *Court* for me that will
> Tottering Favour's slipp'ry hill.
> All I seek is to lye still.

Cromwell, on the other hand, does not seek to lie still—has sought something quite other than this. His valor is called—strange collocation—an "industrious Valour," and his courage is too high to brook a rival:

> For 'tis all one to Courage high
> The Emulous or Enemy;
>   And with such to inclose
>   Is more then to oppose.

The implied metaphor is that of some explosive that does more violence to that which closely envelops it than to what is at a distance from it: ignited powder does more damage to the structure of its magazine than to some wall against which the charge is fired.

The poet points up the complexity of Cromwell's motivation. The forward youth is referred to as one who "would appear," that is, as one who wills to leave the shadows of obscurity. But restless Cromwell "could not cease"; for Cromwell it is not a question of will at all, but of a deeper compulsion. Restless Cromwell could not cease even if he would.

The lines that follow extend the suggestion that Cromwell is like an elemental force—with as little personal will as the lightning bolt, and with as little conscience:

> And, like the three-fork'd Lightning, first
> Breaking the Clouds where it was nurst,
>   Did thorough his own Side
>   His fiery way divide.

Margoliouth tells us that the last two lines refer to Cromwell's struggles after the battle at Marston Moor with the leaders of the Parliamentary party. Doubtless they do, and the point is important for our knowledge of the poem. But what is even more important is that we be fully alive to the force of the metaphor. The clouds have bred the lightning bolt, but the bolt tears its way through the clouds themselves and goes on to blast the head of Caesar himself. As Margoliouth puts it: "The lightning is conceived as tearing through the side of its own body the cloud." In terms of the metaphor, then, Cromwell has not spared the group that nurtured him; there is no reason, therefore, to be surprised that he has not spared Charles.

The question of right, the imagery insists, is here beside the point. If nature will not tolerate a power vacuum, no more will it allow two bodies to occupy the same space. It is amusing, by the way, that Marvell has boldly introduced into this analogy borrowed from physics the nonphysical term *Spirits;* yet I do not think that the clash destroys the figure. Since twenty thousand angels can dance on the point of a needle, two spirits, even though one is a greater spirit, ought to be able to occupy the same room. But two spirits as Marvell conceives of spirits here will jostle one another, and one must give way. Cromwell is all air and fire, "the force of angry Heavens flame." So much for the simile that likens Cromwell to a thunderbolt.

The lines that follow point forward to Cromwell's execution of the king.

> Then burning through the Air he went,
> And Pallaces and Temples rent:
>   And *Cæsars* head at last
>   Did through his Laurels blast.

The laurel wreath, because of its symbolism, was the proper chaplet for a king; the laurel was also supposed to protect against lightning. But nothing can protect the king from this elemental force, and the poem goes on to say, "'Tis Madness to resist or blame / The force of angry Heavens flame." Christopher Hill writes that "the force of angry Heavens flame" was for "Marvell the Revolution . . . 'ruining the great Work of Time.'"[6] Marvell implies that Cromwell is its embodiment. Perhaps this is what Marvell believed in 1650, but the notion is scarcely to be derived from the text of the "Ode."

---

6. Christopher Hill, "Society and Andrew Marvell," in *Puritanism and Revolution,* 362.

The speaker has thus far extolled only Cromwell's energy, his restlessness, his irresistible power against his enemies and even against those who would seek to emulate him. In the stanzas that follow nothing is said about Charles to indicate that he has angered heaven, and, granted the Roman cast of the poem, it would be hard to translate "angry Heaven" into the righteous wrath of Jehovah. If "Tom May's Death" was written by Marvell a few months after the "Ode" (and Hill does not challenge that it was), we note that in that poem "great *Charles*" certainly does not figure as one struck down by God's direction.

The political cause that Cromwell represents is in fact not mentioned until line 82 ("the *Republick's* hand") and line 85 ("to the *Commons Feet*"). Even here the emphasis is on Cromwell's military conquests, with hints of conquests that he may be expected to achieve farther afield. It seems to me that Marvell's approval of a needful revolution that Cromwell has achieved is being read back into the poem out of Marvell's later Cromwellian poems and his later political opinions. This is fair enough if we are aware of what we are doing. But I am here concerned with two rather different matters. First, with the coherence and unity of the poem as set down in 1650 and, second, with what the poem may suggest with regard to Marvell's personal opinions in the summer of 1650.

If Marvell's imagery for Cromwell makes him as ruthless and uncontrollable as a natural phenomenon like the bolt bred in the cloud, Marvell does hasten to make plain that Cromwell was nevertheless a man, a man wonderfully equipped for what he actually seemed compelled to do. Immediately after comparing him to the "force of angry Heavens flame," Marvell adds, "And, if we would speak true, / Much to the Man is due," and goes on to describe his individual virtues and manly achievements. This man has the ability to move—"climbe," the poet writes—from a private life to a public role in which he casts the old kingdom "Into another Mold," bears on his body the deepest scars of the war, brings off cunning feats of deception, and shows himself the master of the "wiser Art" that the statesman requires. The thunderbolt metaphor must not be allowed to mask his virtues as a warrior and as a statesman. For if he sometimes seems a man acting under the influence of an auspicious star, he is not content to be passively directed by its influences. Though it is an "active Star," he himself "urges" it on (line 12).

The reference to Cromwell's "wiser Art" deserves a further comment.

> Where, twining subtile fears with hope,
> He wove a Net of such a scope,

> That *Charles* himself might chase
> To *Caresbrooks* narrow case.

On this point Cromwell has been cleared by all the modern historians except perhaps Hilaire Belloc and Lady Antonia Fraser, who still think that there may be something in the charge. As it turned out, Charles's flight to Carisbrooke Castle on the Isle of Wight did prove to be to Cromwell's advantage, but Cromwell could hardly have known that it would be; and there is apparently no evidence that he cunningly induced the king to flee to Carisbrooke. Royalist pamphleteers, of course, did believe that Cromwell had done so, and used the item in their general bill of damnation against Cromwell. And as the "Ode" shows, Marvell apparently believed it too.

How does the speaker use it here—to damn or to praise? We tend to answer: to praise. But then it behooves us to notice what is being praised. The things praised are Cromwell's talents as such—the tremendous disciplined powers which Cromwell brought to bear upon the king, and his willingness to use any device against him.

For the end served by those powers, the speaker seems to have no praise at all—at least at this point in his poem. Rather, he has gone out of his way to insist that Cromwell was deaf to the complaint of Justice and any pleading of the "antient Rights." The power achieved by Cromwell is frankly called a "forced Pow'r"—a usurped power. On this point the speaker is unequivocal. I must question, therefore, Margoliouth's statement that Marvell sees in Cromwell "the man of destiny moved by . . . a power that is above justice." Above justice, yes, in the sense that power is power and justice can be overborne by power. The one does not ensure the presence of the other. Charles has no way to vindicate his "helpless Right," but it is no less right because it is helpless. But the speaker, though he is not a cynic, is a realist. He knows that a kingdom cannot be held by mere pleading of the "antient Rights": "But those do hold or break / As Men are strong or weak."

In short, the more closely we look at the "Ode" the more apparent it becomes that the speaker has chosen to emphasize Cromwell's virtues as a man and, likewise, those of Charles as a man. The poem does not debate which of the two was right, for that issue is not even in question. Instead, it emphasizes Charles's dignity, his fortitude, and what has finally to be called his consummate good taste. The portraits of the two men beautifully supplement each other. Cromwell is the man of character, the man of action, who "does both act and know." Charles, on the other hand, is the man who knows how to suffer, nobly and without flinching. The contrast is pointed up in half a dozen ways.

Cromwell, though acted upon by his star, is not passive, while Charles is always portrayed as passive. For instance, in chasing away to Carisbrooke, Charles is seen as performing, whether or not he knows it, the part that Cromwell has assigned him to play. (True, we can read *chase* as an intransitive verb—the *OED* sanctions this use for the period—meaning "that Charles himself might hurry to Carisbrooke." But in this context the primary meaning asserts itself: "that Charles might chase [himself] to Caresbrooks narrow case." For this hunter, now preparing to lay his dogs in "near / The *Caledonian* Deer," his earlier royal quarry had dutifully chased itself.)

Even in the celebrated stanzas on the execution, there is a further play on Charles's "acting." In this fullest presentation of Charles as king, he is now in a sense the player king, acting his part. He is called the "*Royal Actor*" who knows his assigned part and performs it with dignity upon the "*Tragick Scaffold,*" "While round the armed Bands / Did clap their bloody hands." Presumably there is no literal blood on their hands, but since not, the only possible meaning is that their participation here involves them in blood guilt for the king's death. Their applause, of course, signifies their approval of what Cromwell is bringing about. But Marvell, with a grim irony, has absorbed even this gesture into his theatrical similitude.

I have read with profit John M. Wallace's *Destiny His Choice: The Loyalism of Andrew Marvell*. It is shrewdly argued, and my own final position on the "Ode" is within hailing distance of Wallace's, but I do have to take exception to his interpretation of some specific passages in the "Ode."

Wallace sees in Charles's conduct an acquiescence in his death which amounted to a renunciation of the crown. Thus Charles made it easier for men like Marvell to feel that they could shift their fealty to Cromwell with something like good conscience. Wallace writes:

> Mr. [L. D.] Lerner has observed that when Charles "bow'd his comely Head, / Down as upon a Bed" he was making a gesture of "perfect acquiescence." The phrase has a happy accuracy and its implications are profound, because Charles's consent to his fate, his willingness to make his destiny his choice, leaves the way open for the conqueror to assume command, and for loyal subjects to accept the new dispensation.[7]

7. John M. Wallace, *Destiny His Choice: The Loyalism of Andrew Marvell*, 79–80.

This seems to me a forcing of the text in the interest of a preconceived theory.

Even more startlingly so is Wallace's reading of lines 61–62, "Nor call'd the *Gods* with vulgar spight / To vindicate his helpless Right." Wallace argues that "in the Ode, by not appealing his case to the gods, Charles has surrendered his right both to fate and to Cromwell, and 'the forced Pow'r' now rules with his permission."[8] If we are to be so literal as this, Charles, of course, did not call upon the pagan gods, nor on any gods, "with vulgar spight" to vindicate him. But he did make a humble and contrite submission of his soul to the Christian God, as his speech on the scaffold clearly shows. Charles's friends, including Bishop Juxton on the scaffold with him, never made any such interpretation of Charles's final speech; and we may be sure that Cromwell did not depend upon it to legitimize his becoming Lord Protector, nor did Charles II believe his father had voluntarily made the crown over to Cromwell.

Christopher Hill believes that Marvell may have been an eyewitness to the execution. His account in the "Ode" well matches that recorded by the Venetian ambassador, himself an eyewitness:

> As they doubted [feared] that His Majesty might resist the execu-
> tion of the sentence, refusing to lay his neck upon the block, they
> fixed into the block at his feet two iron rings through which they
> passed a cord, which, placed on his Majesty's neck, would necessarily
> make him bend by force and offer his head to the axe, if he did not
> voluntarily resign himself to the humiliation of the fatal blow. But the
> King, warned of this, without coming to such extremes, said that they
> should use no violence: he would readily submit to the laws of neces-
> sity and the rigours of force.[9]

The furthest thing from Charles's mind would be to occasion a vain and unseemly scuffle or to call down curses on his captors with "vulgar spight." Marvell's account in the "Ode" apparently accurately records Charles's dignified submission, and that is all—no self-deposition could fairly be concluded from Marvell's account of the scene on the *"Tragick Scaffold."*

The second half of the "Ode" begins with lines 65–66:

> This was that memorable Hour
> Which first assur'd the forced Pow'r.

8. Ibid., 81.
9. Eucardio Momigliano, *Cromwell,* 282.

Note that the speaker frankly calls it a power achieved by force. Cromwell is now the de facto head of the state, and the speaker of the poem, as a realist, recognizes that fact. Henceforth Cromwell is viewed, not primarily as the destroyer of the old state, but as the head of the new. The thunderbolt simile of the earlier stanzas gives way to the falcon simile. The latter figure revises and qualifies what was stressed in the former: in this latter comparison Cromwell again is seen to fall suddenly from the sky, not as a thunderbolt, but as a hunting hawk descending upon its prey. The trained falcon is no wanton destroyer nor an irresponsible one. It knows its master; it is thoroughly disciplined:

> She, having kill'd, no more does search,
> But on the next green Bow to pearch.

The speaker's admiration for Cromwell the man seems to culminate here. Though Cromwell could fairly claim the fame he has won as properly his own, he makes it over to the Commons. He presents to them a kingdom as if it were a "rent" due to them. He has no thought of assuming the crown himself. Instead, he is satisfied with "crowning" each year with fresh victories.

> Nor yet grown stiffer with Command,
> But still in the *Republick's* hand.

Do the words "Nor yet" and "still" hint that Cromwell may not always continue to be so obedient? Perhaps not, but in any case, the compliment to Cromwell derives its force from the fact that Cromwell's homage is not paid out of necessity but is voluntary.

The new state has been founded on the bleeding head of Charles. The speaker takes note of the Roman analogy. He remembers Livy's account of the discovery during the digging of the foundations of the temple of Jupiter on the Capitol. There the Roman architect uncovered a human head, and took the discovery to be a good omen: Rome would some day become the capital of the world.

> And yet in that [grisly object] the *State*
> Foresaw its happy Fate.

But the speaker does not directly apply the happy consequence to the

new English state. Instead he merely predicts even more military successes to be achieved by Cromwell.

> What may not then our *Isle* presume
> While Victory his [Cromwell's] Crest does plume;
>   What may not others fear
>   If thus he crown each Year!

The lines that shortly follow go on to hint at other victories farther
afield, specifically in France and Italy:

> And to all States not free
> Shall *Clymacterick* be.

"Clymacterick" is in this instance to be defined as "constituting an important epoch or crisis; critical; fatal" (*OED* 1b). But in the context it
would seem to also mean "constituting a turning point," as the execution of Charles has proved to do in the history of the English state. In
this context, "not free" means just what? From what will Cromwell
liberate them? From monarchy? Roman Catholicism? The poem only
says specifically that Cromwell might prove "A *Cæsar* he ere long to
Gaul / To *Italy* an *Hannibal*." Yet it is odd to see the Caesar of his *Gallic
Wars* as liberating the Celtic tribes; and it is even more difficult to regard
Hannibal as the liberator of Republican Rome.

George Lord has pointed out that Marvell has used *Caesar* earlier in
the poem to designate King Charles but here to designate Cromwell. It is
an interesting point, and well worth making. But if one wants to argue—I
do not believe that Lord does argue—that Marvell uses this double
reference to signify that the fealty formerly due to Charles has now
passed to Cromwell, there are difficulties. In the first instance *Caesar* is
applied to Charles to indicate that Cromwell dares to strike down the
most highly placed person in the land. In the second instance, the reference is to Cromwell's prowess as a military genius, in which he is specifically likened to the historical Julius Caesar as an invincible military
commander and to Hannibal as another such great general.

Finally, these latter stanzas that celebrate Cromwell the soldier are
pointed specifically toward the imminent Scottish campaign: it is predicted that Cromwell will achieve a smashing victory over the Scots.
Presumably it is with that action specifically in mind that Cromwell is
enjoined to "March indefatigably on."

Before taking up the conclusion of the "Ode," something has to be said about lines 73–80. These two stanzas have stuck in the throats of a number of twentieth-century readers. But could even the most bitterly partisan Englishman of the time—and Marvell was scarcely that—have been able to speak these lines literally? I for one doubt it. Surely they have to be read as uttered with a certain grim irony.

Such a reading well accords with the earlier praise accorded Cromwell—praise for his energy, activity, resolution, and ability to accomplish the mission in hand. The beaten Irish are in a good position to offer sound testimony as to Cromwell's possession of these qualities. Perhaps they are also reliable witnesses as to "How good he is, how just," but could anyone really expect them to answer affirmatively? If a sardonic reading seems out of the question, then I'm afraid that one must concede that lines 79–80 constitute a blemish on an otherwise noble poem.

If, however, the reader finds that they can be read sardonically, then they fit very well into a poem that shows itself to be no mere panegyric on Cromwell, but an unsparing analysis of his character. The wild Irish have been tamed, and now the Pict will no longer be able to shelter under his own "party-colour'd Mind." Such offers no protection against the firm decisions of a man who "does both act and know." Cromwell's mind is not beset with conflicts; it is no teasing mixture of judgments. Perhaps in reality there were, but they do not appear in Marvell's poem. Cromwell's is not only an "industrious Valour," but a "Valour sad." Margoliouth glosses "sad" as "steadfast," and of course he is right. But "sad" can also mean "sober," and I suspect that in this context, with its implied reference to the "party-colour'd" Scottish plaids, it means also "drab of hue."

Up until line 113 the speaker has been content to view Cromwell from a distance, as it were, against the background of recent history. He has referred to him consistently in the third person. But in the last two stanzas, he addresses him directly. He salutes him as "the Wars and Fortunes Son." It is a great compliment, but it is also a considered estimate. Cromwell was fortune's darling, but he was also the son of the wars in that the wars begot him. Had they not occurred, he might, at least the poet seems to say, have continued to cultivate his "private Gardens" and live a life "reserved and austere." It was his performance in battle that speedily moved him up to higher and higher commands until he ended as the most powerful man in the state.

Cromwell is advised to march "indefatigably on" and to keep his sword "erect." The advice is seriously intended, but it carries with it an element of warning as much as it does an element of approval. Those who take up the sword may well perish by the sword: those who have achieved their power by the sword in contravention of ancient rights can expect to maintain their power only by the sword.

What kind of sword is it that is able to "fright / The Spirits of the shady Night"? Margoliouth writes: "The cross-hilt of the sword would avert the *Spirits*."[10] But the speaker has made it quite plain that it is not merely the "*Spirits of the shady Night*" that Cromwell will have to frighten as he marches indefatigably on. It will not be enough to hold the sword aloft as a ritual sword, a mere emblematic sword. The naked steel may still have to be used against bodies less diaphanous than spirits. If there is any doubt as to this point, Marvell's concluding lines put the matter as explicitly as it can be put: "The same *Arts* that did *gain* / A *Pow'r* must it *maintain*." Those arts include not only those of military tactics, but those of the wily statesman as well.

What is the speaker's final attitude toward Cromwell? Before trying to frame an answer, I would stress once more the dramatic character of the poem. It is not a statement—an essay on "why I cannot support Cromwell" or on "why I am now ready to support him." Since it is a poem and thus essentially dramatic in its presentation, it does not eventuate in a decision to take some course of action, but is an act of contemplation. Perhaps the best course, therefore, is to consider its principal characters as one considers the principal characters of one of Shakespeare's history plays. Cromwell is a usurper, but one who demands and commands admiration. But Charles also commands his own share of admiration, and besides that, it is a very serious thing to challenge the "antient Rights" that Charles can claim. We are not allowed to forget that Cromwell's virtues of leadership actually came into being through his assault on those ancient rights. Conversely, Charles's most admirable qualities of character have been given an opportunity for expression only through his defeat and death. The "Ode" is suffused with a sense of honesty, deep insight, and whole-mindedness of the sort that we associate with great poetry.

The characteristic virtues of one man do not cancel out the characteristic virtues of his rival. Rather, they serve to throw into high relief those of his counterpart. On one hand there is the anointed king, who has become such by legitimate succession, a king who is willing to suffer

10. Margoliouth, ed., *Poems and Letters,* 2:239.

for what he believes is right, and who dies with a fitting nobility. On the other, there is a man who is kingly by virtue of his endowment with every natural talent, whose ability to command an army and to govern the state has been demonstrated over and over, who has used his power not for self-aggrandizement, but to serve the Commonwealth. Though lacking a legitimate right to the throne, Cromwell was kingly in every other way. Five years later Marvell was still reiterating that thought. In "The First Anniversary" he says of Cromwell, "He seems a King by long Succession born."

The presentation of this ironic state of affairs is, of course, not the whole import of the poem, but clearly the poem makes much of the contrast presented. But it concludes with a stress on the victorious contender, Cromwell, and with some guarded speculations upon what England's future may hold under Cromwell's leadership. Yet to ignore the references to Charles and his cause would badly distort the poem.

How accurately does the "Ode" reflect Marvell's state of mind in the summer of 1650? The honest answer has to be: I do not know. I have tried to read the poem and to infer what it seems to reflect of Marvell's attitudes toward the events that had recently occurred. But it is probably fair to assume that the ironic contrasts evident in the "Ode" do bear upon the views of Marvell the man at this period. Later events, including Marvell's eulogies to Cromwell, indicate that his views eventually changed radically. About the fact of these changes there can be no disagreement, though there has been much disagreement about the reasons for them and about their exact nature.

Other men's views also changed, including those of the great historian of the Rebellion, Edward Hyde, Lord Clarendon. Clarendon had begun as a moderate Parliamentarian but ended as a Royalist, just reversing Marvell's own shift from Royalist sympathizer to staunch supporter of Cromwell. It may be interesting, however, to compare with the views of Cromwell implied in the "Ode" Clarendon's final estimate of Cromwell.

> He was one of those men, quos vituperare ne inimici quidem possunt, nisi ut simul laudent, for he could never have done halfe that mischieve, without greate partes of courage and industry and judgement, and he must have had a wounderfull understandinge in the natures and humours of men, and as greate a dexterity in the applyinge them, who from a private and obscure birth, (though of a good family) without interest of estate, allyance or frendshipps, could rayse himselfe to such a height, and compounde and kneade such opposite

and contradictory tempers humour and interests, into a consistence, that contributed to his designes and to ther owne destruction, whilst himselfe grew insensibly powerfull enough, to cutt off those by whome he had climed, in the instant, that they projected to demolish ther owne buildinge. What Velleius Paterculus sayd of Cinna, may very justly be sayd of him, Ausum eum quæ nemo auderet bonus, perfecisse quæ a nullo nisi fortissimo perfici possunt. Without doubte, no man with more wickednesse ever attempted any thinge, or brought to passe what he desyred more wickedly, more in the face and contempt of religion and morall honesty, yet wickednesse as greate as his could never have accomplish'd those trophees without the assistance of a greate spiritt, an admirable circumspection and sagacity, and a most magnanimous resolution. When he appeared first in the Parliament he seemed to have a person in no degree gratious, no ornament of discource, none of those talents which use to reconcile the affections of the standers by, yett as he grew into place and authority, his partes seemed to be renew[d], as if he had concealed facultyes till he had occasion to use them; and when he was to acte the parte of a greate man, he did it without any indecensy through the wante of custome. . . .

He was not a man of bloode, and totally declined Machiavells methode, which prescribes upon any alteration of a goverment, as a thinge absolutely necessary, to cutt of all the heades of those and extirpate ther familyes, who are frends to the old, and it was confidently reported that in the Councell of Officers, it was more then once proposed, that ther might be a generall massacre of all the royall party, as the only exspedient to secure the goverment, but Crumwell would never consent to it, it may be out of to much contempt of his enimyes; In a worde, as he had all the wickednesses against which damnation is denounced and for which Hell fyre is præpared, so he had some virtues, which have caused the memory of some men in all ages to be celebrated, and he will be looked upon by posterity, as a brave, badd man.[11]

The resemblance between Clarendon's judgment and that reflected in the "Ode" is at some points so remarkable that one wonders whether Clarendon had not seen a manuscript copy of the "Ode": "Who from a private and obscure birth"—"Who, from his private Gardens, where / He liv'd reserved and austere"; "could rayse himself to such a height . . . by whome he had climed"—"Could by industrious Valour climbe"; and

---

11. Clarendon, Edward Hyde, Earl of, *The History of the Rebellion and Civil Wars in England begun in the year 1641.* The excerpt here printed is item 36 in David Nichol Smith, *Characters from the Histories and Memoirs of the Seventeenth Century,* 139–40.

so on. But I do not want to press the suggestion of any influence of Marvell on Clarendon. Indeed, it makes for my general point to discount the possibility. For what I am concerned to emphasize is that the attitude of the "Ode" is not inhuman in its Olympian detachment, that something like it could be held by a human being of pronounced Royalist sympathies.

The general concern of John Wallace, in a book to which I have earlier referred, is with the development of Marvell's political position. Wallace undertakes to defend Marvell against the charge that he was a turncoat and to discover a consistency of constitutional principles throughout his career. This is an enterprise that engages my sympathies, though in this essay I am primarily concerned with the meaning of the "Ode." Wallace sums up that meaning thus:

> A tentative suspension of final judgment would describe the tone of the ode [rather] than the customary "impartiality". . . . A few years later he could be more positive, and the tone of *The First Anniversary* reflects the difference between a firm but cautions affirmation and a full confidence in Cromwell's ability to rule.[12]

I agree that "impartiality" is not quite the right word. The "Ode" is more than a balancing act. Yet I can't agree that the matter at issue in the "Horatian Ode" is confidence in Cromwell's ability to rule. The matter of concern has to do with Cromwell's *right* to rule—with his constitutional legitimacy. I concede that Marvell was later to settle this matter emphatically in Cromwell's favor. But I can't deduce that from the "Ode."

I prefer to see the "Ode" as an act of contemplation, as an effort to measure the situation. I grant that such contemplation, especially if the events are agonizingly important, is usually followed, sooner or later, by a decision, a choice. Surely this is the normal sequence. The wise man does contemplate the possibilities before he commits himself. But I fail to see even cautious commitment in the "Ode," and if "Tom May's Death" is really from Marvell's pen, then even a few months later Marvell was still uncommitted to the cause of Cromwell and the Parliament.

Since I have quoted at some length the estimate of Cromwell held by

12. Wallace, *Destiny His Choice,* 103.

one of his seventeenth-century contemporaries, it may not be amiss to quote from a twentieth-century historian on this subject, Christopher Hill. One of the most interesting aspects of his essay on the "Ode" is the importance that he attaches to the "tension," as I should call it, that he finds in all of Marvell's best poems. He stresses Marvell's "ability to see both sides"; but Marvell's "double heart" "also shows [in] his attempt to come to terms with and to control the contradictions between his desires and the world he has to live in, his ideals and the brutal realities of the Civil War."[13]

Then, as a preliminary to his examination of the "Ode," Hill proceeds to discuss this tensional quality in some dozen of Marvell's finest lyrics. It is a performance quite extraordinary in a historian, and done with an execution that might excite the envy of a professional literary critic. Among such conflicting forces in the "Ode" he finds "the rather left-handed compliment to Cromwell: his use of force and fraud," and proceeds to assimilate this feature to the total organization of the "Ode."

Hill naturally presents his own reading of the "Ode," and his own version of the later development of Marvell's political views. (This latter, by the way, turns out to be quite similar to Wallace's.) That Cromwell, like Charles himself, dissolved parliament after parliament, and that he eventually became a virtual dictator, does not seem to trouble either Wallace or Hill. In their view, Cromwell served the commonweal well and became the proven instrument of fate, necessity, and the historical process. Marvell, they believe, soon came to recognize this identification and to accept it wholeheartedly. Hence the sincerity of his praise of Cromwell in his poems of the later 1650s.

Nevertheless, Hill, like most of the rest of us, judges these more purely eulogistic poems inferior to the "Horatian Ode," and he offers a reason for this inferiority. "By the time of 'The First Anniversary' and 'On Blake's Victory over the Spaniards,' all Marvell's [inner problems about where his proper allegiance ought to rest] . . . are solved and the great poetry ceases."[14]

In developing this judgment, Hill is working from the poet forward to his poems, whereas I would prefer to work from the poems back to the poet. Nevertheless, Hill and I come to the same basic conclusion. The crucial matter, of course, is that conjectures about the author's state of

13. Hill, "Society and Andrew Marvell," 342.
14. Ibid., 365.

mind should finally be tested against the poem and validated by the poem: it doesn't matter too much from which end we start.

Hill finds in the "Ode" the same tensional character that he believes is the special characteristic of all metaphysical poetry. I would claim that such tension, in various manifestations, is the hallmark of great poetry of whatever kind. I have sought to show how it is to be found in the very fabric of the "Ode."

A Summarizing Epilogue

I have endeavored to keep to a minimum personal and subjective evaluations in my discussions of the poems that make up the preceding chapters. But I believe it is now essential to my purpose to make this epilogue quite personal.

In 1947 I published a book called *The Well Wrought Urn*. I wrote it to show how much intrinsic evidence—what is provided by a careful consideration of the internal structure of the poem, the use of diction, figurative language, tonal shadings, rhythms, and so forth—could reveal about what actually got "said" in the poem as compared with extrinsic evidence, such as that provided by the author's life, the historical epoch in which he lived, and so on.

Thus, in *The Well Wrought Urn* I deliberately played down the relevance of extrinsic evidence. Of course, it would be difficult to eliminate it in its entirety. If you do no more than name the author or date his poem, you have begun to furnish extrinsic evidence. Actually, *The Well Wrought Urn* contains more than a modicum of such evidence, but I had been so restrained in my use of it as to make many a reader believe that I had dismissed all extrinsic evidence. To such readers, I seemed to be saying that the dominant graduate school program for literature was irrelevant to literary criticism.

In 1946, while I was preparing *The Well Wrought Urn* for the press, I published another book, this one entitled *The Correspondence of Thomas Percy and Richard Farmer*. Percy was later to become a bishop in the Church of England, and Farmer, the head of a Cambridge college. But in the 1760s, the period of their principal correspondence, they were simply two young antiquarians who had become intensely interested in the English literature of the late medieval, Tudor, and Elizabethan periods. The letters that I was editing were not very "literary." They were filled with accounts of scholarly researches. Percy and Farmer were examining manuscripts, collecting rare books and rarer pamphlets, identifying authors, and dating works. In short, their subject matter consisted almost entirely of reports on extrinsic evidence relevant to the earlier literature. Percy, Farmer, and their fellows were laying the foundations for what was to be the literary scholarship of the next two centuries.

As for my edition of their correspondence, many a page was composed of some dozen or so lines of the text of a letter supported from below by twin columns of notes in smaller type. My notes were packed with more extrinsic evidence: corrections or further discussions of the work of these pioneer scholars and identification of now obscure eighteenth-century worthies who also had antiquarian interests. Such was the culminating expression of my own graduate studies.

Was I aware of any irony in working almost simultaneously with books so diverse in matter and method? I was not, and I still see no reason I should have been. My labor on each book gave its own kind of satisfactions. Nor would it be fair to say that *The Well Wrought Urn* represented a kind of rebound from the drudgery that working on the *Percy-Farmer Correspondence* entailed. Writing literary criticism may involve its own sort of drudgery. Certainly it can be hard work.

The Republic of Letters needs both kinds of activity. Percy's most celebrated book, *The Reliques of Ancient English Poetry,* nourished the Romantic poets of a later generation. Scott, Wordsworth, and Coleridge so testified. Though Percy, in his old age and nearly blind, apparently never read a line of the poetry of either Wordsworth or Coleridge, and though I can find no evidence that he even heard of them, their debt to him was, nevertheless, a real one.

Yet in spite of the fact that the scholar's use of extrinsic evidence is valuable and is, as I hope the preceding chapters of this book have shown, often quite indispensable for the understanding of a poem, it does not follow that extrinsic evidence avails to solve every kind of problem. To be blunt, one can know all *about* an author and the circumstances under which his poem was written and still not grasp the meaning of the poem. The history of literary scholarship is replete with instances. For example, my discussions of "The Faeryes Farewell" and of "The Grasse-hopper" show how even an impressive amount of knowledge about a poem may fail to yield any real elucidation.

Now is it satisfactory, on the other hand, to argue that true appreciation and evaluation are so hopelessly subjective that one's time is better spent in finding out the "solid facts"—those that are either verifiable or probably true—and then allowing each reader complete freedom to respond tò the poem as he will? Such may seem to be an attractive proposal, and it does embody a solid truth: namely, that each reader must finally appropriate the poem for himself, and that any such personal appropriations will always to some degree be affected by the values, perspectives, and prejudices of the reader. Nevertheless, the "facts" topped off with a dollop of pure impressionism can produce some truly weird results. Usually this method tells us more about the reader's mind and reading habits than it tells us about the meaning of the text he is reading. In any case, the conscientious reader will be chary of imposing on the poem his own personal beliefs and attitudes. He will begin his reading by assuming that the poet knew what he was doing and that the makeup of the poem, even in its detail, will turn out to be meaningful and not empty embellishment.

I trust that the preceding chapters constitute solid testimony to my own regard for the importance of establishing authorship, datings, biographical and historical references, and the specific and sometimes archaic uses of words that make up the poet's text. It was in order to give full scope for the use of historical evidence that I chose for detailed discussion poems written three hundred years and more ago. Yet I must insist that for works of literary art such evidence cannot provide sufficient basis for interpretation and evaluation. Those two activities are closely related, for both are principally based on intrinsic evidence. Think how much "The Faeryes Farewell" would be diminished as a work of literary art if one left out the skillful handling of tone as the Puritan is played off against the Roman Catholic and both against the fairies. Consider also how much a relatively slight lyric such as "The Glories of Our Blood and State" gains in weight from a full awareness of the basic metaphor that works its way throughout the whole poem.

My choice of seventeenth-century poems provided fewer opportunities to demonstrate the use of biographical material. We know so much less about the lives of the seventeenth-century poets than about those of later periods. But enough is available to test the relevancy of biographical information to the interpretation of poems and enough to examine the problem of the poet's sincerity. "An Exequy" and, most notably, the three of Andrew Marvell's best-known poems provide good examples.

Nevertheless, it may be profitable to consider here a little further the poet's proprietorship over the poem that he has created. Some years ago the problem came to a head in the various discussions of what importance could be assigned to the poet's stated intentions in his creation of a poem.

In 1944 Monroe Beardsley and William K. Wimsatt published an article with the provocative title "The Intentional Fallacy." Protests were immediately forthcoming, for if the poet didn't know what his poem meant, then who could pretend to know? Besides, it was insulting to imply that the poet, as a kind of inspired idiot, had no intentions at all. In any case, it was arrogant to imply that his intentions were better left to others to identify. "The Intentional Fallacy" was particularly alarming to the scholarly establishment, for it seemed to call in question the time-honored methods of conventional literary studies.

In 1968 Wimsatt addressed himself once more to the matter of the author's intentions as cited as evidence for the elucidation and evaluation of literary works. The title of this second article, "Genesis: An Argument Resumed," was less provocative than the earlier one, and the argument as developed was accompanied by more concrete illustrations and offered more reservations and qualifications. But Wimsatt's original thesis was fully maintained.

To state it very briefly and in my own terms, poets do have intentions, and of course it is common sense to take them into account when they are available to us. What finally counts, however, are the achieved intentions, not prospective intentions or intentions as later recollected, perhaps recorded in a letter or diary or remembered by a friend as having been told him by the poet. The shaping impulses are indeed important, but *as manifest in the work.* For if poets sometimes write better than they "know," they also sometimes write worse than they think they do. Moreover, poets express not merely the impulse of which they are fully conscious, but those from the unconscious also. In any case, poets sometimes forget, sometimes give partial answers about their intentions, and sometimes deliberately give cross answers to what they evidently regard as crazy questions. Most of all, poets frequently modify their plans as the work develops.

René Wellek's general position on this matter of the poet's intentions as they are recorded outside the work itself is much the same as Wimsatt's, though of course expressed in Wellek's own terms. See, for example, "The Mode of Existence of a Literary Work of Art," which is one of the chapters in *Theory of Literature* (with Austin

Warren), the first edition of which appeared in 1942. Since I have levied upon *Theory of Literature* for the very useful terms *extrinsic* and *intrinsic,* it will be convenient just here to state the matter of intentions, purposes, and plans for the work in terms of the Wellek-Warren account of these two different approaches to literature.

Evidence of the author's intentions as gathered from an examination of the work itself is clearly *intrinsic* evidence, and has priority over every other kind of evidence of the author's plans. To say this is not to declare extrinsic evidence as of no account. As we have seen, it may on occasion provide valuable hints and clues. But whatever such extrinsic evidence may suggest must in the end be tested against the work itself. If the avowed intention cannot be found in the poem in question, what is its worth as evidence for the meaning of the work?

Some of us were charged in the past (and by many today are still charged) with robbing the poet of his own poem, taking it over to interpret it as we like. But a careful concern for the details of the text as written tells quite another story: such a concern bespeaks a true regard for the poet's artistry, and a sincere respect for his art is the finest compliment that most literary artists would want to receive.

Selected Bibliography

Allen, Don Cameron. "An Explication of Lovelace's 'The Grasshopper.'" *Modern Language Quarterly* 18 (1959): 35–43. (Reprinted in *Seventeenth Century English Poetry,* edited by W. R. Keast, 280–89. New York: Oxford University Press, 1962.)

Beardsley, Monroe. See Wimsatt, William K.

Belloc, Hilaire. *Charles the First, King of England.* London: Cassell and Co., 1933.

Brooks, Cleanth. "Literary Criticism." In *English Institute Essays, 1946,* 127–58. New York: Columbia University Press, 1947. (Reprinted as "Marvell's 'Horatian Ode'" in *Marvell: Modern Judgements,* edited by Michael Wilding, 93–113. London: Macmillan, 1969.)

———. "Literary Criticism: Poet, Poem, and Reader." In *Varieties of Literary Experience,* edited by Stanley Burnshaw, 95–114. New York: New York University Press, 1962.

Burghclere, Winifred. *Strafford.* 2 vols. London: Macmillan, 1931.

Butler, Samuel. *Hudibras.* 3 vols. Edited by Treadway Russell Nash, with illustrations by William Hogarth. London: T. Rickaby, 1793.

———. *Hudibras.* Edited and with an introduction and commentary by John Wilders. Oxford: Clarendon Press, 1967.

Chaucer, Geoffrey. *The Works of Geoffrey Chaucer.* 2d ed. Edited by F. N. Robinson. Boston: Houghton Mifflin, 1957.

Clarendon, Edward Hyde. *The History of the Rebellion and Civil Wars in England begun in the year 1641.* Edited by W. Dunn Macray. Oxford: Clarendon Press, 1888.

Cleveland, John. *The Poems of Cleveland.* Edited by Brian Morris and Eleanor Withington. Oxford: Clarendon Press, 1967.

Corbett, Richard. *The Poems of Richard Corbett.* Edited by J. A. W. Bennett and H. R. Trevor-Roper. Oxford: Clarendon Press, 1955.

Cowley, Abraham. *Poems.* Edited by A. R. Waller. Cambridge: Cambridge University Press, 1905.

Crofts, J. E. V. "A Life of Bishop Corbett, 1582–1635." *Essays and Studies by Members of the English Association* 10 (1924): 61–96.

Crum, Margaret, ed. *The Poems of Henry King.* Oxford: Clarendon Press, 1965.

Daniel, George. *The Selected Poems of George Daniel of Beswick, 1616–1657.* Edited by Thomas B. Stroup. Lexington: University of Kentucky Press, 1959.

Donne, John. *The Poems of John Donne.* Edited by Herbert J. C. Grierson. 2 vols. Oxford: Oxford University Press, 1912.

Donno, Elizabeth Story, ed. *Andrew Marvell: The Complete Poems.* Harmondsworth: Penguin, 1972.

Eliot, T. S. "The Metaphysical Poets." *TLS* 1031 (October 1921): 669–70. (Reprinted in *Seventeenth Century English Poetry,* edited by William R. Keast, 22–30. New York: Oxford University Press, 1962.)

Fanshawe, Richard. *The Lusiad, by Luis de Camoens, translated by Richard Fanshawe.* Edited by Jeremiah D. M. Ford. Cambridge: Harvard University Press, 1940.

———. *Sir Richard Fanshawe, Shorter Poems and Translations.* Edited by N. W. Bawcutt. Liverpool: Liverpool University Press, 1964.

———. *Selected Parts of Horace, prince of Lyricks . . . now newly put into English.* London, printed for M. M. G. Bedell and T. Collins, 1652.

Fraser, Antonia. *Cromwell, the Lord Protector.* New York: Alfred A. Knopf, 1973.

Gardner, Helen, ed. *John Donne: The Divine Poems.* Oxford: Clarendon Press, 1957.

———. *The Metaphysical Poets.* Revised edition. Harmondsworth: Penguin, 1966.

———. *The New Oxford Book of English Verse.* Oxford: Oxford University Press, 1972.

Góngora y Argote, Luis de. *Obras Poeticas de D. Luis de Góngora.* New York: Hispanic Society of America, 1921.

The Greek Anthology. Translated by W. R. Paton. Loeb Classical Library. New York: Putnam's, 1927.

Gregg, W. W. *A Bibliography of the English Printed Drama to the Restoration.* 4 vols. London: Printed for the Bibliographical Society by the University Press, Oxford, 1951.

Grierson, H. J. C., and G. Bullough, eds. *The Oxford Book of Seventeenth Century Verse.* Oxford: Clarendon Press, 1964.

Haller, William. *The Rise of Puritanism.* New York: Columbia University Press, 1938.

Hardy, Thomas. *The Complete Poems of Thomas Hardy.* Edited by James Gibson. London: Macmillan, 1976.

Hartmann, Cyril H. *The Cavalier Spirit and Its Influence on the Life and Work of Richard Lovelace.* London: G. Routledge, 1925.

Herbert, Edward. *The Poems, English and Latin, of Edward Lord Herbert of Cherbury.* Edited by G. C. Moore-Smith. Oxford: Clarendon Press, 1923.

Hill, Christopher. "Society and Andrew Marvell." In *Puritanism and Revolution.* London: Secher and Warburg, 1946. (Reprinted in *Marvell: Modern Judgements,* edited by Michael Wilding, 65–92. London: Macmillan, 1969.)

Howell, T. B., comp. *A Complete Collection of State Trials and Proceedings for High Treason.* 21 vols. London, 1816.

Jonson, Ben. *Ben Jonson.* Edited by C. H. Herford and Percy Simpson. 11 vols. Oxford: Clarendon Press, 1925–1952.

Joyce, James. *Ulysses.* New Random House edition. New York: Random House, 1961.

King, Henry. See Crum, Margaret; Mason, Lawrence; Sparrow, John.

Latham, M. W. *The Elizabethan Fairies: The Fairies of Folklore and the Fairies of Shakespeare.* New York: Columbia University Press, 1930.

Legouis, Pierre. *André Marvell: Poète, puritain, patriote, 1621–1678.* Paris: H. Didier; Oxford: Oxford University Press, 1928. (English ed. revised and abridged as *Andrew Marvell: Poet, Puritan, Patriot.* Oxford: Oxford University Press, 1965.)

Leishman, J. B. *The Art of Marvell's Poetry.* New York: Funk and Wagnells, 1968.

Lord, George de F. *Andrew Marvell: Complete Poetry.* Modern Library College Editions. New York: Random House, 1968.

Lovelace, Richard. *The Poems of Richard Lovelace.* Edited by C. H. Wilkinson. Oxford: Clarendon Press, 1925.

Margoliouth, H. M., ed. *The Poems and Letters of Andrew Marvell.* 2 vols. Oxford: Clarendon Press, 1927.

Marvell, Andrew. See Donno, Elizabeth Story; Lord, George de F.; Margoliouth, H. M.

Mason, Lawrence, ed. *The English Poems of Henry King, D. D., sometime bishop of Chichester.* New Haven: Yale University Press, 1917.

Momigliano, Eucardio. *Cromwell.* Translated by L. E. Marshall. New York: Scribner's, 1930.

The Most Ancient and Famous History of the renowned Prince Arthur, King of Britain . . . London: William Stansby, 1634.

The Oxford Companion to English Literature. Compiled and edited by Sir Paul Harvey, 1932. 4th ed., revised by Dorothy Eagle, 1967. 5th ed., revised by Margaret Drabble. Oxford: Clarendon Press, 1985.

The Oxford English Dictionary. 13 vols. London: Oxford University Press, 1933.

The Oxford English Dictionary: A Supplement. Edited by R. W. Burchfield. London: Oxford University Press, 1972-.

Pevsner, Nikolaus. *Yorkshire: The West Riding.* 2d ed. Revised by Enid Radcliffe. Harmondsworth: Penguin, 1967.

Rivers, Isabel. *Classical and Christian Ideas in English Renaissance Poetry.* London: George Allen and Unwin, 1979.

Saintsbury, George, ed. *Minor Poets of the Caroline Period.* 3 vols. Oxford: Clarendon Press, 1906.

Selden, John. *The Table Talk of John Selden.* Edited by Samuel Harvey Reynolds. Oxford: Clarendon Press, 1892.

Shirley, James. *The Dramatic Works and Poems of James Shirley.* 6 vols. Edited by William Gifford, additional notes by Alexander Dyce. London: J. Murray, 1833.

Simeone, William. "A Probable Antecedent of Marvell's Horation Ode." *Notes and Queries* 197 (1952): 316-18.

Smith, David Nichol. *Characters from the Histories and Memoirs of the Seventeenth Century.* 1918. Oxford: Clarendon Press, 1929.

Sparrow, John, ed. *The Poems of Bishop Henry King.* London: Nonesuch Press, 1925.

Thomas, Keith. *Religion and the Decline of Magic.* New York: Scribner's, 1971.

Townshend, Aurelian. *Aurelian Townshend's Poems and Masks.* Edited by E. K. Chambers. Oxford: Clarendon Press, 1912.

Wallace, John M. *Destiny His Choice: The Loyalism of Andrew Marvell.* Cambridge: Cambridge University Press, 1968.

Walton, Izaak. *Walton's Lives of Dr. John Donne, Sir Henry Wotton, Mr. Richard Hooker, Mr. George Herbert, and Dr. Robert Sanderson.* New ed. revised by A. H. Bullen, with a memoir of Izaak Walton by William Dowling. London: George Bell and Sons, 1884.

Wedgwood, Cecily Veronica. *Strafford, 1593-1641.* London: J. Cape, 1935.

———. *Thomas Wentworth, First Earl of Strafford, a Revaluation.* London: J. Cape, 1961.

Wellek, René, and Austin Warren. *Theory of Literature.* 3d ed. New York: Harcourt, 1977.

Wimsatt, William K., Jr. "Genesis: An Argument Resumed." In Wimsatt's *Day of the Leopards: Essays in Defense of Poems,* 11–39. New Haven: Yale University Press, 1976.

Wimsatt, William K., Jr., and Monroe Beardsley. "The Intentional Fallacy." In *The Verbal Icon: Studies in the Meaning of Poetry,* by Wimsatt, 3–18. Lexington: University of Kentucky Press, 1954.

Index